Claim *Your* Light

Unlock Your Capacity to Become
a More Vibrant and Authentic Person

WAYNE BENENSON, PH.D.
BARB HUGHSON, ED.D.

where words connect

Claim
Your
Light

Unlock Your Capacity to Become
a More Vibrant and Authentic Person

Claim Your Light: Unlock Your Capacity to Become a More Vibrant and Authentic Person

ISBN: 978-1-959811-04-6 (Paperback)
ISBN: 978-1-959811-05-3 (eBook)
Library of Congress Control Number: 2022922033

Cover Design: Okomota
Interior Design: Amit Dey
Illustrations: Zac Crawford

Twitter: wordeeeupdates
Facebook: facebook.com/wordeee
E-mail: contact@wordeee.com

Published by Wordeee Beacon, NY 2023
Website: www.wordeee.com

Printed in the USA

Advance Praise for Claim Your Light

"I have read Dr. Benenson and Dr. Hughson's book, *Claim Your Light.* I found their stories and research lighthearted, challenging, and hopeful. Without a doubt, their nuggets about life and healing are sorely needed in this season to help individuals and communities rekindle their light, persist in breaking down mental and emotional constructs that prohibit genuine connections, and risk for the hope of living a wish, fulfilled life. Praises to Dr. Wayne and Dr. Barb for their wit, authenticity, and courage to live aloud."

—Renae McKee (ret. Hospital Chaplain)
Member, Association of Professional Chaplains

"Self-improvement, personal growth—whatever you might want to call it, it's a learning process. One learns how to do things differently in order to get different results. That's what makes this book's approach so powerful. The authors ground their discussion in the discipline of education, providing a framework for self-understanding from which one can consciously decide how to make whatever changes one wants to make. And they combine this theoretical framework with personal stories, application examples and breathwork of how to put the theory into practice in the specific context of one's unique life."

—Peter Theodore, Ph.D., Assoc. Professor Emeritus
Learning, Culture, and Society
Southern Illinois University Edwardsville

"Dr. Wayne and Dr. Barb presented me with a means of gaining a fresh perspective about myself. Through their take on empathy, grit, a growth mindset, and that place of inner quiet, I've learned a different way to set goals and achieve my aspirations. I have a new, practical approach to help me increase a sense of fulfillment in my life. Their question, "What's your soul's hunger?" enticed me to answer it."

—Anna Kato, Ed.D.,
Certified Clinical Hypnotherapist

"Drs. Barb and Wayne combine decades of expertise in education and curriculum development to create the steps necessary to live a more vibrant life. *Claim Your Light* offers a transformative guide to help readers move forward in life by listening to our inner quiet, identifying needs instead of wants, and cultivating the power of empathy, grit, and a growth mindset. Each chapter offers their own examples of concepts followed by an application activity that is designed as a workbook for readers to put these concepts into practice. This book delightfully blends science, research, and theory with practical application and relatable examples that will compel any reader to participate in the journey to find your hidden vitality."

—Lisa Parrott, Ed.D.

"When I finished reading *Claim Your Light*, I realized that it could solve a problem that is threatening nearly every business and not-for-profit organization. Employees say they're working together to achieve the goals while, in fact, they're pursuing their own goals as their top priority. The result is that organizations struggle to succeed while their executives wonder what is making their lives so difficult. *Claim Your Light* helps employees discover new abilities within themselves and enables them to work together as a team."

—Philip Musgrave
Certified Financial Planner

Table of Contents

A Statement About Our Collaboration

Dr. Wayne Benenson and Dr. Barb Hughson believe that multiple perspectives are much better than one to promote sustainable change. To get there, they passionately practice this maxim: honor similarities and celebrate differences. Together they bring a wider set of eyes, based on their different gender, age and clients (teaching parents, kids, or workers how to manage conflict). When relationships are respected, even if they are not understood completely, diverse viewpoints can be heard without a knee-jerk judgment. They are also adept "companion-buddies" who can bring on the calm when frustrations cause a fight, flight, or freeze response. They know that bringing a soothing tone when guiding others through the quicksand of change increases the chance for transformational change to happen.

Foreword

Books on change, both of personal transformative change and systems change, often overpromise and under-deliver. Why? It's quite understandable, really, when one equates the expected change as "better" rather than simply "different." Transformation can sound so enticing if a perception of one's identity, life skills or habits leave much to be desired. Who wouldn't want a radical makeover that replaces mindless suffering with a tonic that magically undoes past conditioning? That's the key, isn't it, serving up a potent tonic to blast past a life on automatic pilot? Happily, Wayne and Barb do not offer up the latest elixir to take away the sting of change. They hold up the notion of curiosity to get to the other shore. The process they describe is not new. It is grounded in ancient wisdom that allows us to move forward with new eyes and fresh resolve.

I was impressed by how they moved the conversation of change from surviving life's slings and arrows to actually thriving, and in turning adversity into opportunities. How does that work? The short answer is, by building capacity. As one increases in their ability to respond to frightful change from a place of vision and compassion rather than ego or self-interest, one's life can be filled with more meaning and contentment. From their educator's perspective, the main question on transformative change boils down to this image: "What if the person standing in the wings, ready to burst on to the stage in a more vibrant way, was simply waiting for his or her cue?" The main point, for me, is the rock-solid sensibility that every person already has all that he or she needs to live a more vibrant life. One moves from surviving to thriving by knowing yourself at your core and being guided by your inner wisdom. The section on consciousness-change, as well as the exercises and questions throughout the book, will be allow a new wisdom to bubble up, a new presence to emerge that is integrated, creative and aligned with one's higher purpose.

Ultimately, the way of seeing and thinking and reflecting upon ourselves and environment asks basic questions about a sustainable relationship with the whole web of life. The last chapter is a fine summary of the general process of self-questioning that gives insight to the more specific questions throughout the book. I especially responded to the I-Thou reference at the beginning of the chapter for it reminds the reader the purpose of a re-examined life is to enter into communion with one's fellow human beings. Buber's I-Thou, I-It, philosophy does that; it takes us out of our own little world to engage with our struggling sisters and brothers around us. I also liked the emphasis on the Key 3: empathy, grit, and growth mindset. Empathy puts us in touch with the humanity in others and in ourselves. Grit means having the courage to listen to what's going on in the conflict between our inner self and the outer world. Grit backs up one's good intentions. Dostoevski said celebrating love in one's imagination is easy; but loving in one's daily life can be gut wrenching. Loving in our daily life, both the personal and the public, and caring about sisters and brothers all over this land, is the how we wake people up to the real game of life? If we do those first two well, empathy and grit, my experience tells me, a growth mindset will follow along. First, we act, embrace the search for personal transformation, then our view of the world changes to help reinforce the new direction allowing each of us to be the person we were meant to be.

Finally, I was intrigued by the blending of academic explanations with literary and cultural examples as well as pop culture gems to appeal to a wide audience. Mick Jagger and Tagore do indeed address common issues of what human life is all about. I also enjoyed the stories Wayne and Barb shared at the end of each chapter for a personal account of self-actualization. By sharing what may be embarrassing or vulnerable they effectively distance themselves from the overly simple, "me-based" popular works on change which can encourage a siloed selfishness. These authors are believable, trustworthy, and accessible. They mix their reactions to the Key 3—of empathy, grit, and growth mindset—with the scholarship of transformative education with a healthy dab of similar perceptions like Buddhist mindfulness and

Maslow's hierarchy of needs. This book will, no doubt, appeal to a broad, basically humanistic, audience. Claiming your light is something anyone can do, humanist or religious (or spiritual), and will draw people who are living half-fulfilled lives, of what Thoreau called "lives of quiet desperation," into new possibilities of personal and professional growth. Wayne's and Barb's final sharing puts the reader in touch with two real people who've had their own transformation—personally and professionally—that they want to share with others. It's a sharing most definitely worth your time and attention.

John Corry
Author and Theologian
Albuquerque, New Mexico

Preface

I need to say this from the start, I've (WB) been a card-carrying member of the self-help movement for years. The whole shebang: books, videos, audiotapes, workshops, FB interest groups, and conferences, among others. My chosen career, education, has played right into this desire for self-growth.

When I first started teaching fifty years ago, the national fad (education is very prone to fads) was continuous self-improvement. Yep, that hooked my imagination big time, through elementary and middle school teaching, and later as a professor teaching preservice teachers. I didn't know it at the time, but I learned one very important sensibility from the self-help movement. It kept popping up in my life like a lyric from a song. That notion, so simple yet so undervalued by the critics of education, is this: encourage a student's potential. It is hard-wired into every teacher's toolkit. Effective teachers (and coaches) know that learning begins when a student feels safe enough to take a risk to stretch himself or herself. Think about it. Did you have a special teacher who made a difference in your life? Was it someone who believed in you even before you believed in yourself? Was it someone who encouraged you to aim high and dream big? This was certainly true for us. My co-author and I both deeply resonate with those education euphemisms such as "igniting the spark to learning" or "not giving up on a student." However, if that was the case for you, or if you want to relive that experience again, we'd like to provide the forum.

The self-help movement cuts through many disciplines, chiefly counseling, business, and religion. However, it has not always been on good terms with educators. Education is lumped in the category of social science, somewhere in the quicksand of "hard" science like medicine and the "soft" mysteries of the arts or religion. As authors, both successful teachers, we were looking for a self-help book that combined the precision and concision of hard science with the warmth and wonder of the softer side of what makes us human. Since we couldn't find a book to suit us, we decided to write one. *Claim Your Light* is what we wanted to read throughout our career. It's an educator's perspective on expanding the human potential in students of all ages. It's about finding that vibe that makes you feel special and then working it until your dream becomes a reality. Educators have a name for that process. It's what draws us to this low-paid, high-demand profession. It's called the "teachable moment." When that learning connection between teacher and student is made—the proverbial "aha" moment—well, nothing compares. This book is our recollection to help you find your teachable moment.

When I was a teenager, I couldn't get enough of the Beach Boys hit "Good Vibrations." It played constantly in my head. Interestingly enough, that tune still plays in my head today. I am attracted to both the beat ("Good, good, good...good vibrations") and its message. Back then, the notion that I had the power to change my vibe was a new thought for me. Imagine that...I could recalibrate my mood, like flipping the channels on the radio dial, whenever my equilibrium had been disturbed. I could alter my attitude when my mood soured. I could get unstuck after a disappointment or setback. Nevertheless, I wondered how and where I could find those good vibrations. This book is about finding your vibration, your most authentic self.

Part of that treasure hunt is recognizing the seeds of your own authenticity. The signs are everywhere but intensely personal: a dream that keeps coming back, a song lyric that plays on a continuous loop in your head, a snippet of an overheard conversation that feels like it was meant just for you. It's fair to ask if these random-but-important connections represent a pipeline to the deepest parts of your soul, or are simply pipe dreams of ephemeral desires.

When I (BH) was beginning my career, I suffered a bit from imposter syndrome. Was my enthusiasm for shaping lives enough to overcome my inexperience? A nagging doubt haunted me. When would I get the chance to teach what my students thought was important as I followed the objectives of what the administrators thought important? Finally, fitfully, I found a way to do both. I could be *both* a teacher and an instructor when I paid close attention to what astonished me. I came to see that I was astonished by my student's quirky humor. I was astonished at their sense of triumph when mastering—finally—a difficult academic skill. And, humbly, I was astonished at their perseverance when sharing one of their life struggles. Claiming your light means you are willing to be astonished and reconnected with your most primal sense of self despite the distractions of the day.

However, the ride to what's genuine and great in your life is often bumpy. Those daily distractions represent both dangers and opportunities on your journey to a more vibrant you. Be mindful of the potholes! The capacity to pry open your most essential self is directly proportional to the amount of friction in your life. Change often occurs when conflict has your undivided attention. It is during those times of strife when you are really paying attention. However, we are not doomsayers. We are only asking, "How much of that conflict is self-imposed by expectations of perfection?" For example, when I am stressed out (BH) my need for order is magnified and I revert to an old habit of wanting to prove myself to the world.

Equally, for me (WB) my stress causes me to worry too much and look for catastrophe around every corner. This creates unnecessary conflict, a burden of suffering on top of the ever present pain. Our experience (and lots of positive psychology studies) suggest that constant stress pushes us to micromanage our life and stifles creativity and flexibility. Cherished notions of perfectionism are hard to sustain, consume lots of time and energy, and lead to diminishing returns. Perversely, our dissatisfaction causes us to look for more ways to be perfect and we become busier and busier, which just feeds this vicious cycle. If you identify with this perfection-trap—procrastinate regularly, feel like you fail at everything you try, and struggle to relax—this book may be a lifeline.

The premise of this book is to learn how to be resilient in the face of adversity; to claim your light. But what does that mean? Claiming your light means to identify with your inner glow, your wisdom. It's your ace in the hole when everything in your life is going sideways. The capacity to recover quickly from difficulties can become obtainable when you regularly practice a "both/and" perspective to conflict. It's important to point out that the conflict is NOT the struggle between the old you and your future ideal. Rather, the conflict points out how willing you are to make new choices in the present moment. What we advocate will probably take you out of your comfort zone. Why? Because it means holding two opposing tensions at the same time. With as much grace and tenderness as you can muster, acknowledge both the unwanted habit and the new norm which is coming into being. For example, if your past is littered with failed attempts at managing your finances, then your new *Claim Your Light* behavior is to both acknowledge, without self-judgment, the unproductive habit, (say, impulse buying) and embrace, without elaboration, the new habit (perhaps, building up your savings account to afford a big-ticket item). Look at the subtitle of this book: *Unlock Your Capacity to Become a More Vibrant and Authentic Person.* That means seeing opportunities hidden in adversity. Resiliency means finding the light amidst the heat. As the songwriter Don Henley describes in his song, "My Thanksgiving," "Sometimes you get the best light from a burning bridge."

The craft of becoming a more vibrant person can happen at either end of a continuum. At one pole your focus is on getting unstuck from negativity. Whatever your self-improvement effort—losing weight, managing money without fear, or attracting joy and compassion in intimate relationships—you won't be successful until you change your thinking and move your mindset from "I can't" to "I can." This book offers a guideline on how to do that through three important keys: Empathy, Grit, and Growth Mindset. At the other end of the spectrum is your calling, your life purpose, your connection to your positive instincts. Are you brave enough to dissolve the barriers to your calling, however scary or vague? To do so involves consciously deciding on what kind of life is most truthful for you. Choosing to claim your light will no doubt bring on more heat as you distance yourself from habitual self-sabotage. To prevent you from getting scorched this book offers a recurring refrain of Listening to Your Inner Quiet to deepen and nurture your shift in consciousness. As you re-imagine the expanded version of yourself, think of these concepts and practices as tools to trigger your soul and allow you to reach and exceed your grasp.

Although the ideas in this book can be used as a stand-alone guide to self-improvement, we have seen more success when it's used as a companion piece for realizing a specific goal. The first part in each chapter is the conceptual piece— the WHAT of transformational change. At the end of each chapter are application activities—the HOW of transformational change. If you are really pressed for time and want a sneak peek at changing your life, just read the application activities.

This symbol marks the application activities section at the end of each chapter.

For those of you who really want to cement your intended change into a stable new habit, we also offer an online coaching call to empower your new intent and to build a community of support which allows the change to stick. For more information, go to our GreatMasters website at: www.greatmastersinc.com. It is our hope that you find value and vitality in this book. May you imagine growing into a fuller version of yourself. May this conscious choice to embrace your best self, ignite your passion and purpose. We honor your courage to do the work that allows you to shine. As you commit to the journey, hold close to your heart these words from Rabindranath Tagore, "Faith is the bird that feels the light when dawn is still dark."

Wayne Benenson, Ph.D.
Barb Hughson, Ed.D.

Introduction

Outer Wholeness + Inner Quiet = Hidden Vitality

C an you imagine growing into the person you were meant to be? Hmm, what an audacious question. There's so much to unpack in this provocative question. What does "meant to be" mean? According to whom? And what nurtures that growth? Who has those magic seeds so I can have my Jack-in-the-beanstalk moment? Okay, okay, perhaps a scaled back question might be, "Can you imagine living your life in a more vibrant way?" Whoa, whoa, wait a minute. My life is already way too complicated and who has time for a social or psychological makeover? All right, all right, let's try one last stab at hooking the golden ring. What if, hypothetically speaking, the "you" that was meant to be was already here, right now? What if that person standing in the wings, ready to burst on to the stage in a more vibrant way, was simply waiting for his or her cue? This anticipated metamorphous is similar to Michelangelo's explanation on creating the iconic sculpture of David, "He was already inside the marble, waiting to get out; I just chipped away the outside stone."

This book is an instructional manual on how to chip away the outside fragments of stone to allow your amazing self to appear, unadorned. It's a guide for learning a process to help you construct a new, more accurate, worldview. This is called process knowledge. It is the cement which makes the social and emotional building blocks of your life stick together. This process knowledge can increase your confidence when taking on long-avoided personal challenges.

But wait, you say, not another self-help book! Do we really need another self-help book fueling a $10 billion per year industry? Not another formula for success: just follow these ten easy steps and you will (fill in the blank… improve your health…lose weight…make a fortune, find your sweetheart…improve your relationships, etc.) in only_____short weeks. Don't miss out on this great opportunity. This pitch works so effectively because it taps into our personal sense of inadequacy to fulfill the latest version of the American Dream. Although the lure of a better life is universal, quick fix remedies usually end up with headache or heartache.

These come-ons work for two reasons. First, they tap into time frames you can't control, namely your stories of past failures or your fantasies of future fulfillment. Real change will elude us whenever we are stuck in a time warp. If we are living, consciously or unconsciously, with a life story dominated by past or future expectations, then we've given away our personal power. The past is gone, the future is yet to come. We only have control in this present moment. Second, these improvement impulses come from an incomplete sense of who we are. That's all about the wicked perfection myth which erodes our tattered image. If only I were more disciplined, a better planner, less fearful in the face of adversity . . . and blah, blah, blah. Perfect is an awfully high bar for us mortals to strive for, let alone reach. So, what to do, what to do? Wouldn't it be a relief to know which steps can give the biggest bang for the buck?

The premise of this book is to share that journey to wholeness in real time and real place. That means reframing the perception of yourself—your new sense of self—with everyone watching. No doubt, your first thought might be: Horrors! No way. How embarrassing. I couldn't possibly do that. And that's the whole point. You get to your new "me" while embracing a new "we." Learning about transformative change while in a supportive community not only keeps you accountable but also allows you to be authentic. When you're honest with yourself and with others you naturally take responsibility for any bumps on the way. So, find a buddy to share your triumphs and tribulations with on a weekly basis.

One more thing. Besides focusing on the present moment and sharing the ups and downs with someone (or someones) in a safe and supportive environment, we must be willing to live with purpose and passion. This is how our best self-shows up. Truth be told, that's the secret of our approach. When we live each day aligned with our deepest values, we discover new veins of resilience. The source of resilience is within us. Everyone has an innate ability to overcome obstacles and become a better version of themselves. That new capability comes when we learn how to recognize our outer wholeness and actively listen to our inner quiet.

Recognizing Our Outer Wholeness to Learning

The most obvious cost of change is the disruption of your familiar stability. It can be so uncomfortable or scary, perhaps even dangerous, to leave the comforts and security of your semi-functioning (or dysfunctional) worldview. Of course, you want to make your dreams come true. But wanting it is not enough to realize your goal. Neither is relying mindlessly on someone else's plan, even one conveniently offered in a book or video. Most of the self-help practitioners come from the fields of psychology, theology, or business leadership. Their expertise is grounded in the long tradition of empirical science, religious scholarship, or marketplace success. Compelling stuff, for sure. What could we educators add that's new or helpful? It is fair to ask what makes our approach different.

Here's our bottom line: we believe that an education model deepens personal and interpersonal relationships. When you sense you are in a trusting relationship it is easier to take a risk to try out new attitudes or behaviors. Think of how you learned to read or ride a bike. Was there a supportive adult who knew how to move you along without overwhelming you? This approach works not only for readin', 'riting and 'rithmetic but also for resolve and resilience. Learning something new rests on three educational foundations: curriculum, instruction, and evaluation. We use these foundations in each chapter as a blueprint for change that sticks.

We are proponents of "whole learning" and believe there are many different avenues to achieve a result. Given so many different roads to success, what vehicle would best allow you to get past the roadblocks and detours? The cornerstone of our Claim Your Light approach is to identify key personal attributes that show how to navigate change amidst the potholes. We call these qualities our Key 3 of sustainable change: empathy, grit, and a growth mindset. We have paired each of these qualities to the framework of whole learning, the ABCs of Affect (heart change), Behavior (physical or body change), and Cognitive (mind change). This merged pairing of Key 3 within the ABCs is the foundation to Curriculum development and Instructional design. They make up the outer wholeness to learning. See, these two wings—the Key 3 and the ABCs—as an upgrade to your basic operating system. It's your new floor supporting the weight of the revamped you. It's what James Clear had in mind when he wrote in *Atomic Habits*: "You don't rise to the level of your goals. You fall to the level of your systems." Finally, we will address the third key of whole learning—Evaluation through reflection—in the "Listening to Our Inner Quiet" section.

Curriculum Development

Curriculum development is the "what" of learning. The descriptions below offer the yin and yang of how to unpack new knowledge and skill and attitude.

1. AFFECTIVE:

- **Heart:** our emotions, feelings, intuitions, perceptions, or moods.

  Empathy connects us to our heart. When we get past the "monkey mind" in our head and remain curious to how others respond to a situation, we are showing empathy. When we are sensitive to the mental state of another person, we are showing empathy. It involves two components: a cognitive understanding of why someone is feeling a particular way and an emotional component of sensing (again, without judging) the feelings another person may be experiencing. When we turn empathy inward, we practice a self-compassion which can reduce emotional barriers to new and unfamiliar change and better allow the transformative process to unfold.

2. BEHAVIORAL

- **Body/Performance:** observable activity; a pattern of action.

  Grit connects us to our body and movement. If we can believe and act on a new image of our self, we are practicing grit. Creating a vision of new attitudes and behaviors toward an old nemesis allow us to stay in the present. By simply acknowledging but not identifying with my demons (e.g., negative body image, feelings of financial insecurity, a sense of personal inadequacy in romantic or professional relationship, etc.) I can sidestep harsh judgment. Grit focuses on perseverance and passion for long-term goals. Our behavioral homework is to increase stamina and to maintain effort despite potential setbacks. Grit turned inward is the practice of continual vigor toward a goal and knowing how to get up (after a setback) when you want to give up.

3. COGNITIVE

- **Mind:** perception, memory, judgment, and reasoning; knowing

  Growth Mindset connects us to our mind. It is a bottom-line understanding that intelligence can be developed. Those with a "fixed mindset" believe that abilities are mostly innate and interpret failure as the lack of necessary basic aptitude. Those with a "growth mindset" believe that they can acquire any given ability provided they invest effort or study. While elements of our personality, such as sensitivity to mistakes and setbacks, can make us predisposed towards holding a certain mindset, we can intentionally reshape our mindset through our interactions. Growth mindset turned inward reframes a daunting task into an interesting game of how proactive effort eventually leads to proficiency.

Think of the ABCs of these Key 3 as the scaffolding around your new behavior. They are the props on an empty stage. The real electricity happens when the stage comes alive with actors and lighting and sound and the palpable energy of audience engagement. Likewise, growth to the more vibrant "you" occurs when all the moving parts are in sync. Just as the members of the audience momentarily suspend belief to allow the reality on stage to capture their imagination, the authors of this book ask you to suspend self-judgment of your deficits or limitations and imagine a different set of beliefs, grounded in a sense of abundant wonder.

The ABCs represents a holistic way to address our basic needs. Feel free to mix and match. People process information in countless different ways. If you are a global thinker, wanting to see the big picture before committing to a course of action, then you might focus on Cognitive and conceptualize your plan toward positive change. Perhaps you are a person who feels deeply. Your focus would naturally go to Affective as you empathize with the personal struggle of someone who has reached a formerly impossible dream. Perhaps you are an action person. You would no doubt find good examples in a Behavioral response as your keen powers of concentration (or stubbornness) to continue, one foot after another, to a new projected goal. It's important to remember that there is no best component of the ABCs. Think of how you overcame obstacles to meet a past challenge, whether it was learning how to drive a car or learning how to be a responsive parent. It's probably safe to assume that sometimes you found success by using your head and other times by leading with your heart. The key to practicing the ABCs of learning is doing what works for you at a given moment of time.

Instructional Design

Instructional design is the "how" of learning. How can new knowledge or skills or attitudes be delivered most effectively? We use a three-step series of questions to keep us on track toward our goal:

> WHAT? This phase identifies the awareness of what is to be learned: What's the problem? What was done in the past that worked? What was done in the past that didn't work? What new commitments can be made?

> SO WHAT? This phase identifies the intervention of what is to be learned: What's your personal learning style? How do you process new information (hearing, seeing, or doing)? How do you learn best in a social context (in isolation, or with another person, or in a small group setting or in large groups, or by using

technology)? Additionally, how many repetitions of new information or skill is necessary to make it routine?

NOW WHAT? This phase identifies the assessment of what is to be learned: What is useful? What defines accountability, that is, assessing emotional and social progress as well as cognitive change? What means are used to evaluate outcomes (tests, essays, presentations, performances, etc.)? What's in the gray area that can't be evaluated, that is, what are leading trends or patterns of new behavior?

If curriculum development is the scaffolding around your new behavior, then instructional design would be the pace you take toward that change. A rule of thumb many teachers use when introducing a new concept or skill is the seven repetitions practice. *It takes seven repetitions of a new learning before it becomes habitual.* This assumes, of course, that the student is paying attention and has a belief that the new learning is important. That plays into another rule of thumb. We have found that it generally takes an adult at least 45 days of conscious attention to change a belief (and longer depending upon age or for how long the limiting belief has been active). These are broad strokes, but they can give you a hint about how long it takes to make lasting change.

Listening to Our Inner Quiet

Learning what sticks is more than acquiring new knowledge or a new bag of tricks. It's important to create a space for reflection, to carefully think about something. Our thoughts—how we interpret our life or someone else's life—are no more than one person's viewpoint in the unified whole of reality. While the thinking mind can be a useful tool, it can also be very limiting when it gets too bossy. Have you ever had a moment when you realized that your mind's insistence on the familiar tried-and-true formulas from your past were actually getting in the way for new change to occur? How can I trust this new belief or behavior? What does this have to do with following dreams or changing habits? Why is it important to go beyond the thinking mind? Einstein had the perfect answer, "We cannot solve our problems with the same thinking we used when we created them." When we reflect on how we process information—educators call this meta-cognition—we shift our consciousness. And as philosophers and poets and singers attest, we have a better chance to shift our consciousness when we replace active mind with quiet mind.

A quiet mind is a less reactive mind. Wisdom bubbles up when we are still, simply looking and listening without a predetermined agenda. The theologian Paul Tillich once observed that our world and ourselves would be changed for the better if we would seek "more rest for the soul." If we are really serious about making real changes in our life (and in our world) we have to quiet the inner noise, the "monkey mind," of our thinking. Regular periods of active silence in our daily routine allow us to recognize information from our intuition as well as our logical, reasoning mind. Getting in touch with our inner quiet awakens new connections to how we see thorny challenges. Stillness is where creativity and solutions to problems are found. From this vast reservoir a new consciousness is born, weaving fragments of old ways of being with a newly emerging curiosity to new interpretations.

This new consciousness represents a shift from "either/or" thinking to "both/and" thinking. When we move our attention to a wide-angle lens beyond perceived limitations (fear _and_ wisdom, worry _and_ acceptance, resistance _and_ non-resistance, etc.) we can expand the outcomes available to us. That makes it much easier to shift from a rigid mindset to a more fluid mindset. That's the keyhole to sustainable change.

Paradoxically, as we tap into our inner quiet it becomes easier to embrace our perceived limitations. As we exchanged our back stories while writing this book, we recognized a truly perverse truth: when we acknowledged our vulnerability, honestly and without judgment, we found a deeper strength, a hidden wholeness. So many times, one of us would stare at the other in disbelief and say, "Really… I thought I was the only person in the world to have such feelings." Such revelations are important way stations on our journey to transformation. We want to share our mistakes and triumphs as we've come to terms with the necessary potholes on the road to change. In the last section of each chapter we will share our own "vulnerability" stories as we struggled to resolve personal conflicts in our life. It would be incredibly shortsighted and inauthentic to suggest changes toward sustainability without sharing our own "muddling through" process. Hopefully our "aha" moments can be conversation starters for you. This process of removing self-imposed boulders in our way is hard work. There's no playbook. However, it's less scary when we muddle through together.

The Last Word

We've come full circle. How do we take the leap to that new life we want? Our answer is by showing up and learning how to consciously build personal capacity. How? By embracing an educational model of outer wholeness and inner quiet. This is how we hold sacred our hidden vitality. The mythologist Joseph Campbell nailed this truth, "I don't believe people are looking for the meaning of life as much as they are looking for the experience of being alive." If that's something which grabs your attention, then read on. The following chapters will outline best practice applications of our Key 3 Approach of empathy, grit, and growth mindset with reflective activities to quiet our ever-active mind. This is how we can get unstuck and reclaim our light. This is the "juice" of our getting and keeping the change we seek.

A final caveat. In our collective experience—70 years of teaching between us—we've had remarkable success with helping students increase their confidence. To be clear, most of the students who followed our Key 3 Approach didn't really believe, deep down, that it would work for them. However, they became converts after the fact. Perhaps that's the real power of claiming your inner light. We offer a reliable template to build your capacity to become a more vibrant and authentic person. All we ask of you is your sincere effort to go beyond the well-worn groove of your comfort zone. Fear not what lies ahead. We will companion with you. We have taken our own medicine and we will share some of our own stories of how we worked with the Key 3 to turn gristle into greatness. If you are ready for the re-energized you to show up, then let's get to it!

Application Activities

Outer Wholeness + Inner Quiet = Hidden Vitality

Authors Note: Reflecting on the ideas from each chapter can help you grow into the vibrant person you already are. Truth be told, your greatness has always been present, however you may not have always been conscious of it. These application activities can sharpen your focus and remind you of your connection to your deepest and most authentic self. It is time for your moment on center stage. See yourself there. Use these activities as a springboard to your imagination and commitment to get you there!

1. Self-awareness is a first step to shifting your energy and increasing emotional intelligence. Describe a situation where you reacted in a way that was not effective or creative. Describe what you were thinking. How were you feeling?

2. Self-awareness is a conscious knowledge of one's own character, feelings, motives, and desires. Jot down some initial thoughts on how you can improve your self-awareness and expression of your emotions.

3. Rate yourself on these conditions which can lead to increased awareness. Describe your behavior by circling the appropriate number from the following code:

   5 = very present in my regular behavior

   4 = somewhat present in my regular behavior

   3 = neutral or no opinion

   2 = hardly present in my regular behavior

   1 = rarely present in my regular behavior

1 2 3 4 5   A. FLEXIBILITY - can generate many different ideas rapidly

1 2 3 4 5   B. TOLERANCE OF AMBIGUITY - comfort in situations where everything is not in order

1 2 3 4 5   C. SPONTANEITY - responding to situations directly rather than following someone else's plan

1 2 3 4 5   D. ADVENTUROUSNESS - a love of exploring the world around you and exploring the inner self

1 2 3 4 5   E. BOLDNESS - acting confidently and humbly if opinions are challenged

4. Given your rating in #3 above, in what areas would you give priority to increase and sustain your self-awareness? Why?

5. Envision a new way to manage and control your emotions. Change the caption of the cartoon below to reflect your top priority to manage your emotions.

   "Agenda item 1: My need to _____"

6. List 3 intentions you can set for yourself at the start of each day to bring you to a place of heightened self-awareness.

7. Who can you enlist to help you provide observations of how they experience you expressing and managing your emotions?

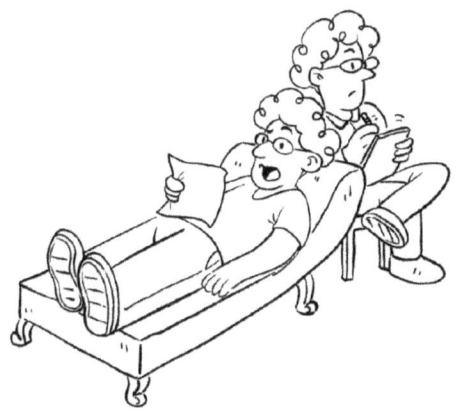

Agenda item# 1: My compulsive need to be in charge.

CHAPTER ONE

Identifying Our Needs

"You can't always get what you want, but sometimes you might find, you get what you need."

—Mick Jagger

One of my [WB] first jobs was as a counselor for a national weight loss franchise. I would hold half-hour weekly sessions on healthy eating habits, positive self-image, and proactive behavioral tactics to prepare my clients to deal with the evil binge gnome during those festive times like going out to eat or holiday celebrations. Yet, in my opinion, we started the weight-loss process on the wrong foot; we focused on their wants more than their needs. Before I met my clients our sales team already asked them how many pounds they wanted to lose and why they wanted to lose the weight. A great majority of these weight loss customers were women, and they nearly always had a quick response, a desired end result: to fit into a lower-size wedding dress, to be able to wear a bikini for a summer vacation, to look fabulous for a family reunion. However, they had more difficulty when I asked them nearly the same question, a process question, in the counseling room, "Why did they need to lose the weight?" Better put, "What needs were not being met at their current weight?" A lot of awkward silence and squirming generally followed my questions. It was incredibly painful for them to identify the real needs that motivated them to spend time and money to lose weight. A surprising number admitted that no one from their immediate circle had asked them that question before. Initially, I was startled. Why? What might happen if you opened up and revealed what you really needed? However, after hearing the same story told again and again, with a different cast of characters or in a different setting, I began to see a pattern: "loving women," that is, women who care for others more than themselves, have no needs. (The analogy for men was: "standup men," that is, guys who didn't want to appear weak, have no needs.) What is this craziness, I thought, which prevented someone from sharing a genuine human need? They all had the same answer. They were afraid that they would be judged harshly if they were open and honest. They were scared that a significant other in their life would reject them, tell them what's wrong with them, that they were too sensitive, needy, or demanding or _____ (fill in the blank). The message was plain. It's better to be oblivious to our needs than have to deal with the pain surrounding those needs. Silent suffering seemed preferable than having to deal with a negative opinion from family or friends who disapprove of going off script. Given these challenges, how can authentic needs be verbalized without prompting a reactive "like/dislike" response?

ABCs of Noting Needs: Affective
From Hard-Hearted Awareness to Soft Hearted Awareness

If deep change is really going to take hold, we need to let go of our past understanding of success and reach for a new world of being. This new world of well-being starts when we soften our heart and cultivate prosperity thinking. This means being ruthless but not harsh in examining deeper beliefs about ourselves and our world. A hard-hearted awareness focuses on deficit thinking; the voices in our head are what we heard from significant others from our past: "You are too fat." "You are too skinny." "You are too bookish." "You are too dumb." "You are too controlling." "You are too lazy." The childhood adage, "Sticks and stones can break my bones, but words can never hurt me," is just plain wrong. Words from someone we trust can pierce through a well-armored heart. In the face of certain condemnation, it takes loads of courage to take a risk to open one's heart and be vulnerable.

On the other hand, a soft-hearted awareness focuses on abundance thinking; the voices in our head come from the place of possibilities in this present moment. Perhaps they are the faint whispers from our childhood yearnings, perhaps they emerge from the wellspring of our imagination: "You are strong." "You are flexible." "You are a good problem-solver." "You are thoughtful and intuitive." It's all the perception, right?

Given entrenched beliefs and habits which limit self-correction, how can we move from "either/or" thinking to "both/and" thinking? The trick, of course, is accepting both versions of the heart simultaneously, even if it's only for a moment. How can this be possible?

Guided Imagery

The pathway between these two worlds has been known for ages. We practice it whenever we take a long deep breath to calm ourselves. Just one breath will shift your attention from your mind to your body and help you get centered. Another name for this focusing practice is meditation. Although the word can scare people off, meditation is what we do to dial down our mind, away from outer concerns towards an inner condition of spacious awareness. It's one of the best tools we have to balance our emotions, soothe our physical discomfort, and become attentive to the peace of the present moment.

But it's often too challenging to meditate without a formal practice or teacher. One useful alternative is to do guided imagery. This involves listening to someone (or from a prerecorded meditation on audio or video tape) who sets a tone that allows you to imagine an alternative perspective. From a calmer place that cooped-up sigh can be released. In that moment of expanded awareness, it's easier to mentally let go of unproductive thoughts and feelings. In that more peaceful place, you can rehearse strategies to increase your coping skills. Guided meditation creates a receptive environment for new mental imagery. We can recommend two excellent online audio sources for guided meditation. The first comes from Chopra Center for Wellbeing (http://www.chopra.com/ccl/guided-meditations). Through a variety of offerings, the listener can shift to a place of "balance, healing, transformation, and the expansion of awareness." Another excellent series of guided meditations comes from Tara Brach (https://www.tarabrach.com/guided-meditations/), who blends Western psychology with Eastern spiritual practices to create room in our inner life for a compassionate engagement with our world. Hint: guided meditations offer an array of gateways. Pick a topic that resonates with your most immediate need (e.g., healing, dreaming, gratitude, letting go of control, awakening abundance, etc.), and do it often enough to get the desired result. These audio versions generally last about ten minutes. Many people begin and end their day listening to a guided meditation. Either solo meditation or guided meditation can help us feel the contours of our needs without becoming enslaved to them. A little goes a long way and…the benefits can be subtle and invigorating!

ABCs of Noting Needs: Behavioral

Okay, let's take stock. Assuming that you feel empowered enough to open your heart a crack and entertain the possibility of softening some core beliefs around your affective nature, what temporary scaffolding can be erected to accommodate the changes? That scaffolding to fill the gap between your present state (what is) and your desired state (what can be) is your PNA or personal needs assessment. The first step in making an attitude adjustment is to dream about new realities. The second step is to scheme for those realities. Keep in mind these criteria as you design your plan:

1. Define, as specifically as you can, your most pressing need.

2. Gather and analyze relevant data to create new routines.

3. Set priorities and determine how you will evaluate success.

4. Establish a schedule of sub deadlines and incentives.

So, let's take this model for a spin around the block. One popular needs assessment is the SWOT analysis which is often used as a planning or review process in education, business, and governmental settings. SWOT stands for Strengths, Weaknesses, Opportunities, and Threats. The basic process involves gathering information, personal or organizational, about intended outcomes within a set time period. A simplified version of the SWOT organization process might involve these steps:

*   Members representing different interests of an organization share celebrations and concerns for

several meetings, each lasting a minimum of 90 minutes.

- A list of successes and failures of the organization over the past year is generated. Limited discussion follows, focusing on understanding what's really going on but not dwelling too long on any one feature.

- Based on the understanding of the organization's strengths and weaknesses, members develop a list of external opportunities and threats.

- Members brainstorm ideas to maximize strengths and minimize weaknesses to increase opportunities and neutralize threats.

This needs assessment works well for individual outcomes as well as organizational needs. For example, imagine using the SWOT approach for weight loss: identify a specific goal (lose 25 - 30 pounds to fit into that lower-size dress), gather information from a variety of sources (from MDs, nutritionists, exercise coaches as well those who know your weight yo-yo history); identify strengths and weaknesses (what worked and didn't work in the past); determine criteria for success (daily meditation on that cute outfit you saw online, or chugging a glass of water whenever you cheat) and finally, making a decision of what an acceptable outcome looks like (what a small triumph looks like even if you do not achieve everything from your original goal). And, of course, celebrate any new attitude or behavior that now become a routine part of your life!

ABCs of Noting Needs: Cognitive

A final stock-taking. If you are willing to allow yourself a "both/and" perspective of conflicting feelings toward change and you have a sound plan to reach your goals for hard-to-change needs, then that's that, right? Why would you need anything more? And you would be right . . . for the short term at least. What happens, however, when (and it's most often "when," not "if") you relapse? What will you do when an unforeseen obstacle becomes bigger than your imagined strategy to overcome it? To prepare for these nasty little surprises, be willing to replace rationalizations with hard questions.

Asking a focused question is one of the ways to bring enhanced awareness when you've fallen off the wagon. Questioning exposes our basic curiosity, our innate desire to know how something works. It's that spirit of questioning that led to Maslow's Hierarchy of Needs. In 1943, Abraham Maslow, a developmental psychologist, published a paper describing how human motivation moves through a particular pattern. He identified a hierarchy of needs, now represented as a pyramid, with the more basic needs at the bottom and the highest needs of self-actualization at the top. The bottom four layers of the pyramid contain the most basic levels of human needs. He labeled these fundamental human needs as "deficiency" needs. If these needs are not met the individual will feel anxious and tense. Once these needs are met the individual will strongly desire the secondary or higher-level needs. Listening to your internal questions can give you a more realistic assessment to your most present needs. To use the weight loss example, you will have a vastly different response to a "surviving" question (e.g., If I lose a lot of weight and see myself as more attractive, will my husband become jealous?) than a "thriving" question (e.g., If I lose a lot of weight and see myself as more attractive, will I try for that promotion)? Both questions may bring up fears; however the first question is a threat to your status quo and the second question is an opportunity to further your dreams. Use the Hierarchy of Needs as a perception check to your real needs.

Maslow's Hierarchy of Needs

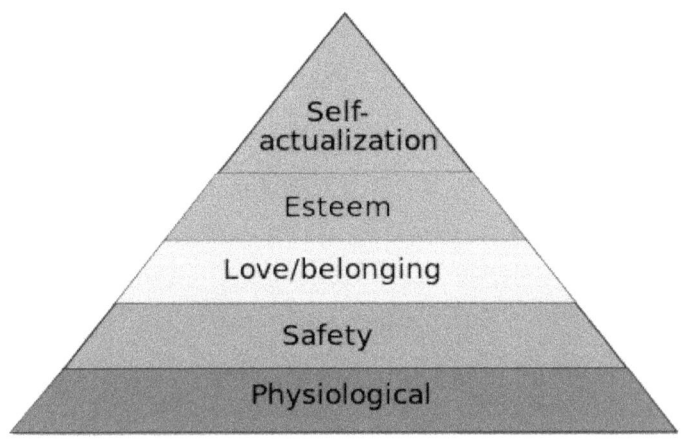

One: Physical/Survival Needs

Food, water, air, sex, and sleep are primary psychological needs. These needs must be met before any other needs are met. When our physical/survival needs are not met it creates extreme and irrational fear. Our most primitive or basic fear is dying.

Level Two: Safety/Security Needs

Protection from physical elements (cold, heat, wind, rain), and freedom from fear of harm to our bodies, minds and emotions are safety/security needs. Humans have a need for structure, order, and personal boundaries. Routines and rituals keep us feeling safe and secure.

Level Three: Love/Social Needs

The need for love is both psychological and physical. A need for affection is also a need to belong. When we identify with a group, the group helps define who we are. An example would be our ethnicity or our political affiliation.

Level Four: Appreciation/Self-Esteem Needs

The need to achieve, to be productive, to master skills, all lead to a healthy sense of competence. Recognition from others for achievements lead to feelings of self-worth, self-love, and self-confidence.

Level Five: Self-Actualization Needs

The need to recognize self-worth, potential, and the value each person brings to a greater global community is self-actualization. When you take full accountability of your needs it becomes easier to let go of taking anything personally. What others say or do is a projection of their reality. Self-actualization is the ability to acknowledge your needs, however awkward and become the best version of your authentic self.

The difference between wants and needs is slippery. The answer may simply be in the eye of the beholder. I (WB) conducted an interesting lesson on wants and needs with my undergraduate college students who were preparing to become elementary school teachers. I put them in groups of four at six separate tables. I passed out an envelope with the same contents to each table. In the envelope were slips of paper describing common items or activities (e.g., milk, chocolate milk, pencil, computer, going to elementary school, going to college, etc.). The task for each group was to put all of the items on a "T Chart" with two headings: Wants on one side and Needs as the other side. However, they had to reach group consensus before they made their selection. At the end of this task, they had to draft a definition of wants and needs to which they could all agree. As you might have guessed, the activity produced a loud and raucous exchange. The lesson ended with a class discussion on the criteria for perceiving a want or a need. My personal favorite, "A need is something you gotta have, no questions asked."

Given the challenges in defining a need, we advocate using targeted questioning to bring a more conscious awareness to a perceived deficiency. For instance, if a reorganization at work reduces the monthly income of the primary provider, it's likely that it would affect each member of the family differently. The chief breadwinner might feel challenged at Maslow Level 4 and ask, "How can I be more productive to feel a healthy sense of competence?" The chief caretaker might feel challenged at Level 2 or 3, wondering, "How can I protect my family from potential physical and psychological shortages?" The change in family dynamics might also affect the children adversely. If routines change abruptly, they may become anxious or have irrational fears characteristic of Level 1: "How come Daddy (or Mommy) isn't home at night like (s)he used to be? Does that mean (s)he doesn't love me anymore?" Again, asking each family member questions about their wants and needs levels the playing field. Being aware of multiple perspectives can ease anticipated anxieties that may bubble up.

Listening to Our Inner Quiet

How can we quiet our mind to discern the magnetic pull of wants and needs? The first step is to pay attention to how thoughts arise. The mind can play tricks on us because it is constantly hungry for food. It is not only insatiably on the hunt for food for thought, but also food for identity. The mind's appetite is voracious; it feeds on the food of our ego. Every time you say "I" or "me," you are referring to the ongoing story of your life, your likes and dislikes, your fears, and desires. This sense of who we are is conditioned by past deeds and future hopes. Since it is not anchored in the present it is rarely satisfied for very long. That voice in your head never stops speaking.

When you notice that voice and respond to the cascading thoughts nonjudgmentally it's easier to pay attention to the energy around the thoughts. For example, reframe the intensity of, "I am so frustrated by my boss when…" to a more bare bones, "Frustrating thought arising, stage left. Take a deep breath or two and let it go." When I give my full attention to this moment (and not digress to an obsessive retelling of past grievances or fantasize about future relief from a suffering) I can break out of my self-constructed ego jail.

Intentionally focusing on my inner quiet world—taking a walk, doing tai chi or yoga, practicing conscious breathing—puts me smack dab in the present moment. In the midst of a deepening stillness, my mindset automatically shifts. I can consciously choose how to respond to those persnickety wants bubbling up. Being aware of right now, this very minute, can free me up to address my condition more fully—what I really need—without a whole lot of emotional baggage. Whew! What a relief.

Dr. Wayne's Story

> I'm a foodie, a card-carrying member of an informal but universal club of food narcissists. I came

by my affliction honestly. My mother, born and bred during the Great Depression, felt compelled to make sure her children had enough to eat… even if they weren't hungry! Her unrelenting focus on food security reached legendary status in my family. She perfected what she called the "dart technique." Whenever an unsuspecting victim had his or her mouth open (my sibs and I were a talkative bunch so that was often), she deftly applied a *blitzkrieg* maneuver and stuffed our gullet with half-inch squares of bologna. To this day I hate bologna! Unfortunately, a habit of a want-disguised-as-a-need took hold. Food is both my sustenance and addiction. Whenever I feel blue there will ALWAYS be something from the pantry or fridge to sooth my tattered nerves. Properly speaking, my problem is not with food itself but with mindless binging of food. The process is invariable: Something upsets me and— Bam! —the switch to my volition suddenly shuts down. My mind just clicks off and I totally absolve myself of any responsibility of what my body does next. So, of course, overeating became the norm. I've struggled with my weight and body-image nearly all my adult life. Regretfully, I've passed on these impulsive habits to my children. Even after several abdominal surgeries, it's still an effort for me to limit the portion size of my favorite foods.

So, what's my Rx? I don't know, it's still a work in progress. Here's my latest needs assessment to limit portion size. I call it my 20/20 plan. Twenty minutes into a meal, I stop eating, and ask out loud if my hunger has been satisfied. Then I wait for 20 minutes (drinking water allowed) before I answer the question. If I am still physically hungry, I can eat, albeit slowly. If I am merely psychologically hungry, I wait another 20 minutes (drinking water expected) before answering another set of questions, "Where am I on the Maslow Hierarchy?" "What non-food remedy would plug the need?" Does my plan work? Honest answer: I have good days and bad days. What encourages me, however, is that I am becoming more conscious of my behavior, and I shut down less often than before. Truth be told, I am both glad and sad at my progress, glad that I am gaining control of my life and sad that it has taken me this long to put the brakes on. Sigh.

Dr. Barb's Story

I have been obsessed with my physical appearance my entire life. Being a dancer for over two decades meant a fine tuning of what a dancer's body should look and feel like. One extra ounce on my frame and I could not get my leg as high in ballet class or be centered for that triple turn. It was palpable. The good thing is that I never turned to eating disorders or use of diet pills. I did not always eat what was best or enough food to really sustain my dancing body as a healthy machine.

We live in such an appearance-obsessed world. Stand in line at any grocery store checkout and you'll see magazines graced with the latest Hollywood stars or famous people who all look fabulous and un-aged. This is not reality. Photoshop is an amazing tool but one that threatens our perception of real life, real issues, and yes, real bodies and faces. We are a quick-fix society and want the youthful look, now and forever. Healthy eating tips are standard fare during cooking demonstrations on television talk shows. Exercise classes abound. The plastic surgery industry has taken on a life of its own. My cognitive, rational brain knows this well. However, my heart and emotional brain lean too far in the opposite direction way too often. Do I eat like a bird on many days? Absolutely. Do I obsess over one more walk in the day just to take off more fat cells? You bet. In thinking about wants and needs it is important to ask the big and unnerving question, "Can I be healthy, and happy?" It took a tragedy for me to see how much I take good health for granted. When a dear friend was paralyzed in a biking accident a few years ago, it shattered my world. A once vibrant friend lost his ability to do simple tasks. Being obsessed with my looks seemed so trivial in the face of his life-changing accident. My superficial wants turned into deeply felt needs. I kicked body obsession out of my life. I developed more gratitude for what I have and can do with my current body. Do I still struggle with the look? Yes, I probably always will. However, now when I look at Maslow's Hierarchy I am drawn toward the need of love for others and an appreciation for a strong self-esteem. Healthy living comes from making good decisions, especially around the value of a healthy and strong body, not one that must 'look' good.

Application Activities
Identifying Our Needs

1. Reflect on a current situation that is a challenge for you. Is this challenge a high concern? What is the unexpressed need?

2. Think about some of the reasons why this need is not being met? What parts can you change? What parts can't you change?

3. Think about a time from your past when you were dealing with a challenging (or seemingly impossible) situation. How did you resolve the problem? Or, alternatively, think about someone you know who has dealt with a challenging situation. How did she or he resolve the problem?

4. What would your life look like if your needs were met, and the challenge was no longer an issue? Sketch out an image of the new look to your life.

5. Complete the following:

   In order for my specific need (briefly state your need) to be met,

   _____

   Here's what I will do:

   _____

   By this date:

   _____

6. When I fall off the wagon in completing my plan to meet this need, I will do these three things:

   1. (An action, perhaps a smaller task, I know I can complete)

      _____

   2. (A feeling or affirmation that rewards honest effort, especially during stressful moments)

      _____

   3. (A reach out to my "helper buddy" and say):

      " _____ ."

CHAPTER TWO

Empathy: Caring About Others to Promote Self-Care

"You never really understand another person until you consider things from his point of view... until you climb inside of his skin and walk around in it."

—Harper Lee, To Kill a Mockingbird

"I am he as you are he as you are me and we are all together."

—The Beatles, I Am the Walrus

"Me. We."

—A poem by Muhammad Ali

For over twenty years, I (BH) have been a mediator in a court-referred family dispute center. Happily, the courts have recognized that issues of child custody are better resolved by parents than by judges or juries. Unfortunately, the prevailing "win/lose" mindset of the judicial system all too often results in settlements rather than durable agreements. Regrettably, a large percentage of these settlements eventually fall apart. What's the difference between the two? A settlement represents a "power-over" outcome; accept my last offer... or else. A durable agreement, on the other hand, represents a "power-with" commitment to a win/win solution. The foundation of a durable agreement is mutuality in a relationship. For example, how can parents attend to the welfare of their child(ren) despite the bruised feelings between spouses? The trick of a seasoned mediator is to move the frame of reference of those in conflict from me to us. By listening fully for that mutual emotional space in each party, their nonverbal presence as well as their verbal exchange; a skillful mediator can shift a defensive monologue to a more productive dialogue. A vital key in mediation is to empower the disputants to recognize win/win possibilities even during a tense negotiation. How? By filling the empathy gap.

Empathy emphasizes the "relate" part of relationship. Simply, it's the connection to the emotional state of other people. In a mediation, there are many ways to telegraph empathy, both verbally ("I get how you feel.") and nonverbally (maintaining nonthreatening eye contact, physically leaning in, or offering affirming gestures). When mediation works, there is a magic moment called "getting to yes." Hard walls become tenuous bridges. Despite the feeling of standing on quicksand one disputant puts down his or her guard long enough for the other disputant to do the same. In this place an awkward silence can dissolve into healing tears; name-calling morphs into sharing what's truly important. Empathy changes the nature of their relationship from adversarial to non-adversarial. The tension in the room softens. For a brief moment they are able to put themselves in another's shoes and experience the events and emotions of the other person from their perspective.

However, the transition from me to we is often tenuous and fleeting. The shaky feelings come from holding two divergent world views at the same time. On one hand the world is seen as a very scary place, full of lurking dangers. It's a dog-eat-dog world, so get yours before someone else does. From this perspective, self-interest is the common-sense bottom line. On the other hand, the world is seen as a beautiful place, full of wonder and promise. It's a loving place, a world where you do unto others as you want them to do unto you. From this perspective, care for self and others is the bottom line.

Both views vie for our attention: a Me-world with competition and aggression as the social norm vs a We-world with cooperation and altruism as the social norm. The tension in that mediation room comes down to which norm to trust.

Since both conditions exist simultaneously within us, how can we attend to our own needs and make ourselves available to the needs of others? The short answer is to recognize the "both/and" possibilities of our needs. Think again about Maslow's Hierarchy. The lower four levels of Maslow's Hierarchy reflect a needs deficit. Something is missing in an individual's life: clothing, shelter, safety, friendship, self-esteem, etc. However, at the highest level of Self-Actualization an individual focuses more on assets than deficits. One's highest needs are satisfied by relating meaningfully with others. That's the ABC of empathy. The ability to understand and share the feelings of another can only come when we understand and share our own "Me/We" needs.

The WHAT of Empathy

To better understand the unpredictability of accepting different motivations (self vs other), social scientists describe empathy from two perspectives: affective empathy or cognitive empathy. Affective empathy, sometimes called emotional contagion, is the capacity to respond with appropriate feelings to the emotional state of another person. This kind of empathy has a plus side and a minus side. Obviously, there are benefits to both parties when someone shows care and compassion for another person. However, without conscious awareness, affective empathy can be harmful to someone who has been traumatized and doesn't wish to be emotionally retriggered. In such cases it's important to manage empathy through cognitive means in order to ensure a sense of safety.

Cognitive empathy, sometimes called perspective taking, is a conscious drive to accurately recognize and understand another's emotional state. However, this can be a slippery slope. For example, how is empathy different from sympathy or compassion? A sympathetic individual has feelings of care and understanding for someone in need but does not share his or her emotional state with the sufferer, "Oh, Dorothy is hurting in a bad way. I feel so sorry for her predicament." A compassionate individual shows care and understanding for someone in need and can share in their emotional state, "Oh Dorothy, I hear the pain in your voice." An empathetic individual is able to mirror another person's emotional state and offer non-invasive support, "Dorothy, I sense your pain. How unsettling. What do you need and how may I help?"

Some of this empathic connection is physiological. In the last two decades neurological research has identified mirror neurons, specific places in the brain that produce empathic responses. When we experience pain certain areas of the brain fire up. The same area of the brain also lights up when we see someone else going through the same experience. For instance, if we see someone stub their toe or fall off a bike we might wince because we can sense that pain ourselves. That unconscious reaction is caused by mirror neurons firing in our brains. These neurons fire whether the action happens to us or happens to someone we're watching. The discovery of mirror neurons was a significant breakthrough because it revealed that our brains have evolved in a way that understands the emotions and intentions of others, not just as a thought but also as a feeling.

However, there is a downside. Too much empathy can be harmful. An unbalanced emotional connection can severely strain a relationship. For example, narcissism is a defect of affective empathy but not cognitive empathy. A bipolar condition is a deficit in cognitive but not affective empathy. Autism and schizophrenia contain deficits in both cognitive and affective empathy. Psychologists have identified an extremely toxic behavior known as the "empathy trap." It is a negative perfect storm in a relationship where someone with pronounced antisocial tendencies preys on an individual with high levels of empathy in order to get his or her own way. The result: Bullying behavior from the predator and emotional paralysis from the victim.

It's fair to ask, "What is a safe way to practice empathy? While remaining alert to the dysfunctional triggers of affective empathy we can ask ourselves about ABC factors that can give us some control of our cognitive empathy responses. Dr. Dan Siegel, a mindfulness researcher, coined the term "Window of Tolerance" as a zone of arousal in which a person is able to function most effectively, especially following adversity."

During crunch times when the empathy response shuts down, his advice is to refocus our awareness. What are our body signs (e.g., tension) or cognitive signs (ex: mental fog) or heart signs (e.g., defensiveness)? After refocusing, we can ask ourselves about a word or phrase which would be helpful? Again, how do we move from me to we?

The SO WHAT of Empathy

The "So-What?" question asks: Can empathy be taught and learned? How does the understanding of another person's feelings translate to actual behavior? According to Edith Stein, a German phenomenologist, empathy can be facilitated, but it cannot be forced to occur. What makes empathy unique is that it happens to us indirectly. When empathy occurs, we find ourselves experiencing it, rather than directly causing it to happen. That makes the act of empathy unteachable through traditional didactic lessons. Instead, promoting mindful attitudes and behaviors such as self-awareness, nonjudgmental positive regard for others, good listening skills, and encouraging self-confidence are important steps in generating empathic awareness.

Such skill-building in empathy is rapidly becoming part of the required curriculum for teacher training. Most teacher preparation programs focus on a teacher-centered training of knowledge, skills, and dispositions. However, a movement is afoot to emphasize the teacher-student relationship. A consortium of local politicians, educators and social service leaders in Seattle published *The Road Map Project.* They recommend balancing relationship-skills and interpersonal development with academic skills. Teaching affective skills alongside cognitive lessons has another benefit for students—self-empowerment. The Ashoka Network of Changemaker Schools (https://startempathy.org/changemaker-schools/) support children as change makers who drive positive change in their culture.

Although the jury is out about how empathy can be learned, there is an emerging consensus on how to tap into our full empathic potential in everyday life. Bottom line: learn how to read the cues of another person's emotional and social intelligence. How? One clue comes from SEL (Social Emotional Learning) studies. These researchers measure the behavioral aspects of empathy through verbal cues (ex: emotionally charged words) and nonverbal cues (ex: voice expression, facial reactions). They identify the landscape through these questions:

1. Can I pay attention? Can I witness, without projecting, a feeling in another person, however challenging, with curiosity rather than judgment?

2. Can I validate that feeling without editorializing, i.e., "I can see you're really angry" rather than "There's no need to be that angry."

3. Can I practice compassion, with others and with myself?

According to the latest neuroscience research, the ability to empathize is already wired into our brains. It is an in-built capacity for stepping into the shoes of others and under-standing their feelings and perspectives. What is necessary to activate it is an awareness of how to get there. The "Now What?" section will explore how we can boost our empathy level.

The NOW WHAT of Empathy

Almost everyone can learn to be more empathic, just like we can learn to ride a bike or drive a car. Let's start with a warm-up exercise. Simon Baron-Cohen, a British Professor of Developmental Psychopathology, suggests paying close attention to "reading the mind in the eyes." Given someone's "look," what word or words would you choose that best describes what that person is feeling or thinking? Going a step further, there are three simple but powerful strategies for unleashing the empathic potential that is latent in our neural circuitry.

1) Make a habit of "radical listening"

Marshall B. Rosenberg Ph.D., psychologist, and founder of Nonviolent Communication, emphasizes the importance of radical listening. Listening carefully for people's feelings and needs gives them a sense of being heard and understood. Let people have their say, hold back from interrupting, and reflect back what they've told you, so they know you were really listening. Radical listening can have an extraordinary impact on resolving conflict situations. Rosenberg points out that in employer-employee disputes, if both sides literally repeat what the other side just said before speaking themselves, conflict resolution is reached 50% faster.

2) Look for the human behind everything.

A second step is to deepen our concern for others by developing an awareness of how we are all connected to each other. Can we be mindful of every person behind routine actions. For example, when sipping your morning coffee, think about the people who picked the coffee beans and those who brewed the specialty blend. Likewise, when you button your shirt, consider the labor behind the label. Think of all the people involved in the supply chain making clothes possible. It is precisely such mindful awareness that can spark empathic action, whether it's buying Fair Trade coffee or becoming available for conversation with the person who cleans your office. It's about recovering the curiosity we had as children.

3) Practice living in someone's shoes through perspective-taking or fantasy.

Don't steal their thunder. Avoid the tendency to problem-solve or editorialize with empathy response, "OMG, how upsetting" rather than "What a stupid boss. When that happened to me, I did this." Affirm their emotional tone: "Wow, that seems harsh," rather than "Well, what did you expect?" Taking a bird's-eye view not only provides an alternate point of view, but gently encourages a shift of mindset to unexpected options.

Another way to show perspective-taking is through a flight of fantasy. Think of a teenager who zones out in electronic games or in romantic fantasy novels. By constructing an alternate reality, the besieged adolescent can find satisfaction in the world of their own making. The key for both types of perspective-taking is to imagine yourself in a similar place, real or imagined, and, for a brief instance, see yourself in that particular situation.

Empathy in Relationships: I and Thou

The consciousness necessary for empathy to be activated is very similar to the ideas of the Austrian-Israeli philosopher Martin Buber wrote about in his early 20th century classic, *I and Thou*. The theme of this book is existence as encounter. He explained this philosophy using the word pairs of "I-It" and "I–You" (or I-Thou) to denote relationships describing different modes of consciousness and interaction. Buber believed that there are two fundamental ways for us to be in the world: as subjects relating to objects (I-It) or as subjects relating to subjects (I-You). An "I-It" existence is a monologue; an individual treats other things, people, etc., as objects to be used. An "I–You" (or I-Thou) existence is a dialogue; the relationship stresses a mutual, holistic existence of two beings. Buber identifies the potential of I-Thou simply and directly, "All real living is meeting. Every person born into the world represents something new, something that never existed before, something original and unique .... If there had been someone like her in the world, there would have been no need for her to be born."

What is the link between empathy and I and Thou? Both recognize the possibility of mutual connection at a deep level when dealing with personal and interpersonal conflicts in our life. When our emotional capacity is stretched to the limit—on our last good nerve—we have a better chance to become replenished when we engage actively with another person. We seek to create a larger container. How can "we," not just "me" get through this situation? An individual exhibiting empathy shifts and responds with his or her whole being to a shared reality, from an I-It duty to an I-Thou kinship.

Interestingly enough, the emotional and empathetic skills one brings to an I-Thou relationship can shift the consciousness between two (or more) people in mutually beneficial ways. Sometimes it may be necessary to pretend to act with empathy, especially when you feel antagonistic to a person. A psychologist who trained hostage negotiators reported the unexpected effect of "faking" empathy. Hostage negotiators are trained to act empathetically toward the hostage taker in order to establish the rapport necessary to influence him or her to give up and not hurt anyone. In fact, the negotiator most likely despises someone who holds a woman and her baby as hostages. What's interesting is that after a couple of hours many negotiators actually start to feel some empathy toward the hostage-taker as a result of "acting" empathetic. When empathy skills are a standard part of relational interactions a higher consciousness is achieved which brings the possibilities of a more authentic relationship.

Listening to Our Inner Quiet

How do we quiet our mind enough to let the magic of empathy unfold? One way is to listen, really listen, to another person deeply, carefully, and non-reactively. Deep listening can bring stillness into a relationship. No relationship can thrive without the sense of spaciousness that comes with stillness. But true listening is rare. Instead of listening we generally use the wait time to rehearse our response. While the other person is talking, we may be evaluating his or her words as we prepare for our come back. Or we may not be listening at all...we're just lost in thought. Instead, we can go beyond the words and empathize with the other person by allowing a space of conscious presence to arise as we listen. In that space the other person is no longer perceived as an "other." In that space me becomes we, joined together in one awareness, one consciousness.

A moment of real attention can be enough to change the quality of the relationship. As I look and listen to the person in front of me, momentarily suspending the screaming prejudices of my culture or tribe, I pay attention to the stillness that surrounds both of us. That stillness—perhaps only two or three seconds of my undivided attention—is enough to go beyond the roles we play. What emerges through this act of conscious attention is my unconditioned self, my essence, my I-Thou. This flash of shared stillness acknowledges an energetic connection between us. This empathetic moment opens up a space for a more receptive realness. One plus one equals one.

Dr. Wayne's Story

The setting: my office...or maybe an online chat. The cast of characters numbers two: me and my doctoral student. The purpose: jumping through seemingly impossible hoops on the path to completing a dissertation. My challenge: setting a high bar for quality work without overwhelming the student. My student's challenge: reaching that bar, in spite of all the distractions and fears...the monkey mind screaming, "This is too confusing. How much more do I have to endure of this endless parade of procedural hurdles?"

I've had the privilege of being a dissertation chair to over two dozen students. A doctoral degree is the gold standard of a discipline; it's the capstone of an academic career, a peek into generating new knowledge in the world of research and...it's devilishly hard work. Therein lies the dilemma. My doctoral students, mostly women between 35–55 years old, are high achievers. They're used to getting A's. However, what worked so well in the classroom (where a syllabus described course content and grading criteria) often falls apart when they have to create their own content in an original piece of scholarship. Old demons haunt them, "Am I really up to challenge? Am I good enough to get to the finish line?" It's an unspoken fact that only half of the students who pass their Comprehensive Exams at the end of their doctoral classes actually complete their dissertation. The first real test of their mettle comes as they prepare for their proposal hearing. The cornerstone of the proposal is a defense of their hypothesis or research questions.

What exactly are the variables to be measured? Their writing and thinking needs to be tight, precise, concise, and clear. That task can be quite daunting; many, many drafts happen before they pass muster. In that excruciating rewrite process, they share their doubts with me. They often feel overwhelmed with a palpable sense that, at any moment, they are about to speed off a nearby cliff, one which only they can see. My job is to listen and affirm and offer a non-anxious presence. I acknowledge their feelings, "Yes, this place you are in right now is uncomfortable and disruptive. And it's OK to be right where you're at." I remind them of how they achieved earlier milestones, similar academic cliffs, which at the time also looked too steep to climb. I assure them that their bout of insecurity is a temporary madness all graduate students experience. We both take a deep breath. Slowly I become aware of my face morphing into a mischievous grin as I comment, "Say your full name out loud." Pause. "Now say it again, only this time add 'Dr.' on the front side. Go ahead now." Their body relaxes. An involuntary chuckle follows. They tentatively try on the expanded version of their soon-to-happen professional title. They sigh or shake their head in amazement. We both smile as we feel the contours of this strange place. Empathy matters.

Dr. Barb's Story

When sitting with clients in a mediation setting, unexpected things happen. Although it's not often the norm, a special opening can occur when a client is able to converse in a non-confrontational way. Many clients going through a court–ordered mediation for divorce or child custody battles tend to be on high alert. Emotions run high and deep. Tempers can get out of control when parties have no way to manage or understand the magnitude of their loss. In the face of quick changes being thrust upon them they often feel as if the rug is being pulled out from underneath. Mediators have to be alert in helping clients recognize transformational possibilities during the negotiation.

During a recent session, a couple came in to discuss parenting issues. However, not much progress was made due to unresolved feelings about their divorce. They were distracted. Who pulled the plug on the marriage? Fingers wagged. Judgments flew. Their deep, though invisible, wounds made it hard to negotiate the necessary pieces of the custody puzzle. Mom was talking briskly telling me what was best, in her view, for the girls. They needed solid emotional support. Her delivery was brittle and repetitive, as if she were talking to herself. Dad sat next to her, silent, seemingly a million miles away. I glanced at him and noticed tears streaming quietly down his face. His eyes showed a deep sadness and fear. Mom finished her story. I turned to dad and asked what was happening for him at that moment. He poured out his heart. A wrenching sadness and overwhelming sense of loss filled the air.

What was going to happen to him and his relationship to the girls? I encouraged mom to connect to that emotion as well. Hot tears flowed from her eyes. They both looked so fragile. An emotional dam had burst. They expressed their deep sorrow for a relationship gone sideways. Yet, until that moment, neither of them had acknowledged or discussed this powerful shared feeling that had a vice grip on them. The logistics of endless paperwork and court dates prevented them from getting to what really mattered to them. Talking about the radical change about to happen in their children's lives impacted these parents profoundly. In that raw moment, they each felt the other's pain. Empathy matters.

Application Activities

Empathy: Caring About Others to Promote Self-Care

1. Describe someone you know (or someone from history) who you believe exhibits great empathy. What personal qualities define empathy? Note the origin and meaning of the word empathy. The suffix -pathy means "feeling" or "suffering." The prefix em- means "within" or "inside." So, empathy is the ability to understand and share the feelings of another. The prefix a- means "not" or "without." So, apathy is a lack of interest, enthusiasm, or concern. To have the most possible empathy (and therefore the least possible apathy) means you feel the feelings of another with the greatest accuracy and effort. On the other hand, to have the most possible apathy (and the least possible empathy) means you are not accurate in describing the feelings of someone else, or it's not a priority for you to care about someone else's

feelings. Both empathy and apathy are contagious, that is, they spread from one person to another by direct or indirect contact.

2. Recount a story on the Empathy/Apathy continuum. Perhaps you showed empathy toward a co-worker who was experiencing a distressing situation, in an office culture that disregards negative or conflictual expressions of feelings. Were the empathy/apathy responses contagious? On a continuum of 1 to 10 with 10 being "High Empathy" and 1 being "High Apathy," what number was your feeling toward the co-worker? What were the feelings of most of the other workers in the office to the co-worker? Was it hard to find common ground? Why or why not?

3. Use your response above to discuss the perspectives of other parties. What number would you give your boss on the Empathy-Apathy continuum? A new employee? Why?

4. How might this perspective sharing exercise shift your attitude about how to practice compassion in a conflictual environment?

5. Describe an incident where you (or someone else in the office) practiced "radical listening," that is, letting people have their say, without interrupting and with a short summary afterwards about what they told you, so they knew you were really listening.

6. Timing and sincerity are so important in demonstrating empathy. Explain a personal encounter when a mistimed remark or a perception of not really caring caused your empathetic response to blow up in your face. Do you relate to the cartoon below? How?

We know just how you feel.

7. Describe a situation where you felt empathy but did not share it. It could have been about abuse to an animal or a child or a graphic image of violence from a television news report. What feelings welled up in you?

CHAPTER THREE

Grit: Persistence in Spite of the Obstacles

"It's not that I am so smart.
It's just that I stay with problems longer."

—Albert Einstein

"One isn't necessarily born with courage,
but one is born with potential. Without courage,
we cannot practice any other virtue with consistency.
We can't be kind, true, merciful, generous, or honest."

—Maya Angelou

A few years ago, when The *Lord of the Rings* movie trilogy was all the rage, I asked a colleague to explain what all the fuss was about with Hobbits and Wizards. He looked at me as if I had lost my mind. After he saw that my lack of enthusiasm made me as pitiable as Gollum, he exclaimed in an exasperated sneer, "Frodo is just an ordinary guy who steps up when he has to. That gives me hope." His identification with the hero of the story is a reminder of the power of grit to pursue a goal over a long period of time. In *The Lord of the Rings: The Fellowship of the Ring*, the first book of a three-volume set of adventures in the mythical Middle Earth, a Hobbit named Frodo begins a dangerous quest. His adventures take him to places of unimaginable beauty and terrifying anguish. He keeps on against all odds, struggles and suffers, often fails, yet perseveres. The tale is so vivid that the reader metaphorically becomes Frodo and experiences his adventure in a deeply personal way. As Frodo discovers the internal resources to fulfill his quest, the reader can imagine tapping into his or her own inner resources to reach a personal goal despite the setbacks.

What's behind the driving force which fuels this power of grit? The key word here is "drive." Persistence and tenacity are not new concepts; nevertheless, grit is now a hot topic in psychology, business, and education. What are the factors beyond normal ability which pushes someone to persevere? Angela Duckworth, a Professor of Psychology at the University of Pennsylvania, is a leading researcher on the subject of grit. She believes that "zeal" and "persistence of motive and effort" are the most crucial components of grit. In a 2007 study, she and her colleagues described grit as "perseverance and passion for long-term goals." But what does it really mean to have true grit? The most obvious answer is showing up, again and again, for a particular task, just because it is important to you. In the end, what drives success is not being exceptional but exhibiting a special blend of passion and long-term dedication toward achieving a goal. Grit is not about the falling down when misfortune blows you off course. It is the getting up again…and again and again.

The WHAT of Grit

Professor Duckworth's team measured grit by looking at one's consistency of passion over time. That could be an idea percolating for a long, long time, fueled by an incessant pursuit to bring that idea to fruition. Or an action, dreary to some but utterly captivating to a person with grit. Individuals who were more successful and influential than their counterparts typically possessed specific traits of enhanced effort. While ability was still critically important, these individuals also possessed "zeal" and "persistence of motive and effort." Individuals high in grit were able to maintain their determination and motivation over long periods despite failure and adversity. Their passion and commitment towards a long-term objective were the overriding factor that provided the stamina required to "stay the course" amid challenges and setbacks.

Essentially, a person of strong grit saw the race as a marathon, not a sprint. What motivates such enhanced effort? What activates the inward drive to reach your dream? The short answer: passion. In study after study of successful people, in all walks of life, passion and purpose were identified as the most important qualities that lead them to success.

Passion and drive distinguishes someone with grit. What stimulates your passion? Think for a moment of a time when you were passionate about something, when it was the sole focus of your attention, intention and action intertwined. Think about what you did to reach your goal, despite the naysayers and obstacles along the way. No doubt you followed a particular order to reach your goal. Those who have learned to focus their passion engage in a three-step process to reach their goal:

1. What do you believe to achieve your dreams? For example, do you believe you are capable of planning and implementing a plan to reach your goal? Do you believe you have enough resources (money, time, support system, etc.) to get the job done? And, ultimately, do you believe in yourself to get to the finish line?

2. Do you accept the conditions necessary to make this dream come true? If unanticipated changes create new conditions, can you revise your expectations to get to your goal or to find your soul's calling? And, tellingly, do you have a Plan B if initial intentions or arrangements go astray?

3. Have you integrated the consciousness necessary for success? Are you attracting the attributes (internal fortitude, a strong desire to find the right pieces of the puzzle, the ability to pivot, when necessary, etc.) to accomplish your purpose? For example, if

your goal is to lose weight or develop a healthier and stronger body, are you doing something every day to make that happen? Integration means applying yourself in those areas where you have control so your effort can increase your competence.

A longer answer about passion and purpose point to courage and resolve. What inner resources empower the strength of character necessary to get to your finish line? Character education is quite popular in public schools these days as a way of dealing with bullying and developing positive self-esteem. Sadly, however, most schools do not have an adequate budget to provide an effective curriculum and instruction to walk the talk of character education. Good intentions are reduced to putting up inspirational slogans throughout the school building (ex: "The difference between ordinary and extraordinary is that little extra.") It's simply not enough to tell students to "buck up" to overcome a lifetime of unproductive habits. A more helpful approach would be to teach this affective skill as they do cognitive skills. It's a matter of taking students where they're at, recognizing how they got there, and caring enough to invest the time and energy to help them move on. Most teachers lack the resources and incentives to help students find their true grit.

The SO WHAT of Grit

Grit involves maintaining a goal-focused effort for extended periods of time, often while facing adversity. Folks with true grit have the self-discipline to control their impulses and pursue what they think is right despite temptations to abandon it. But impulse control does not fully account for how long people persist at something in the absence of positive feedback. To find out how top performers operated, Professor Duckworth interviewed accomplished people in various fields—sports, sales, publishing, entertainment. What distinguished high performers was largely how they processed feelings of frustration, disappointment, or boredom. When others took challenging feelings as a sign to cut their losses and turn to some easier task, high performers did not. They seemed to believe that struggle was not a signal for alarm. This key insight—change the belief about delaying when to quit and one changes the behavior about success—was the foundation of her research. Effort beats talent. Period. So, success comes with effort, effort, effort.

Yet in our obsessively results-oriented society few people want to see the private toil of that effort. Centuries ago, Michelangelo observed, "If people knew how hard I had to work to gain my mastery, it would not seem so wonderful at all." Professor Duckworth comments that it is nearly impossible to find "effortful, mistake-ridden, repetitive deliberate practice" on YouTube. Grit may be essential, but it is not attractive. The key to routinizing this extra effort has to do with applying specific values that help people succeed. Deliberate practice is grounded in the ability to work hard toward a goal and stick to it in the face of adversity and setbacks. It is the resilience to rebound after failure, the inclination to do one's best even in the absence of obvious external rewards, and the willingness to delay gratification.

These nested values create conditions which can turn a perceived threat into an opportunity. Professor Duckworth writes of growing grit from the inside out by combining perseverance and passion within a nest of Interest, Practice, Purpose, and Hope. In their book, *Performing Under Pressure: The Science of Doing Your Best When It Matters Most*, Hendrie Weisinger and J. P. Pawliw-Fry identify a COTE of armor—Confidence, Optimism, Tenacity, and Enthusiasm—on how to handle pressure situations. In this book, we offer the Key 3 of Empathy, Grit, and Growth Mindset to meet your particular challenge that undermines success. Are one set of these nested values preferable to another? Not really. Notice, however, what they have in common. They all skew to a positive orientation, to an "I can" mindset. But what happens if there is no passion nor commitment to sustain these conditions? What if the optimal conditions to nurture grit are thwarted by negative environmental factors such as poverty, social and political oppression, or psychological constraints (PTSD)? What then?

Before we can look at solutions, we need to understand the limits of grit. Is grit a personality trait or a learnable skill? A major implication of Professor Duckworth's work is that grit is a skill: one can learn it. Schools and districts around the country are currently working hard on creating curricula and evaluation measures of grit. But psychologists say grit isn't a skill. Rather, they believe it's a personality trait, driven by some unknowable combination of genetics and environment. The search for a scientific way to describe personality traits goes back at least to the 1930s. But in recent decades, psychologists have settled on a group of overarching personality dimensions known as the Big Five: conscientiousness, agreeableness, extroversion, neuroticism, and openness.

Many psychologists place grit as a subset of conscientiousness whose components include organization, self-control, thoughtfulness, and goal-directed behavior. Herein lies the rub. Her research, grounded in education, suggests that grit is a learnable skill. Psychologists say grit is not something that's necessarily open to change, especially in adults. Even though the jury is still out on the potential of grit, the authors of this book are more interested in practical applications. What are some useful tools to move individuals from where they are to where they want to be?

One organization has attempted to turn those practical ideas into deliverables. The Rising Stars Foundation (https://risingstarsfoundation.org/) has set out to measure and build grit through The Gritter Test for high school students seeking entry into the college of their choice. The Gritter Test Score (https://www.gritterscore.org) is designed to measure two things: 1) a student's ability to learn; and 2) his or her willingness to use that ability. It does not measure IQ, Emotional Intelligence, or knowledge. The priority for them is the student's awareness of what he or she knows and what to do when he or she doesn't know. Students are measured on their ability to detect accurately their own mistakes and to seek help in understanding and correcting them (www.therisingstarsfoundation.com). Gritters grit it out. They may get down when things don't go right but being down doesn't mean being out.

That tenacity is being able to overcome limited or "siloed" thinking (more on that in the next chapter on growth mindset). Those who have specific strategies for dealing with unexpected disruptions can better deal with setbacks; they have an arsenal of tactics to use in challenging situations. For example, they have the ability to break down a single problem into several bite-size mini-questions that provoke creative problem-solving opportunities and builds critical thinking. Although grit is not tied to intelligence and is not domain-specific (that means a person may recognize and exhibit grit in a career, but not in a hobby), the gist of grit can be applied. Learning how to sustain effort over the long haul requires some time to reflect on past behaviors in order to reframe challenges or barriers to achieving a goal. That involves a different way of perceiving obstacles. What are some empowering and nonjudgmental ways to rethink or reimagine how to stay persistent?

The NOW WHAT of Grit

Do you know someone who possesses a dogged determination to succeed? Perhaps it's someone fighting the battle for an unpopular cause or someone who endures one rejection letter after another before finally getting a "right-fit" job or seeing someone cope with a medical challenge. What kept them going? If you could get inside this person's head, you might get a clue to how their thinking propels such persistent behavior? How do they translate good intentions into appropriate choices? An excellent book has been written on how to free ourselves from the conditioned responses of our past, *The Ten Commitments: Translating Good Intentions into Great Choices* by Dr. David Simon. The premise of the book is to turn away from a "commandment" mentality to a "commitment" mindset. For example, the commandment Moses gave against graven images is transformed into a personal commitment to authenticity; the commandment to observe the Sabbath becomes a commitment to relax.

The shift from a commandment mindset to a commitment mindset gets at the heart of what causes limiting beliefs. Most people believe that the cause of their unhappiness come from external forces, "I'm depressed because I am in a loveless marriage," or "I am getting an ulcer due to an overbearing boss." However, if you dig a bit deeper, you'll find some semi-conscious internal voices suffocating your creativity, enthusiasm, and joy. How can we release those restrictive demons? Dr. Simon, a neurologist now associated with The Chopra Center, offers two insights that can expand your perception of Self. The first is to commit your whole self to action. When you make a commitment, you dedicate the entirety of your ABCs to the task: you align your observing heart (Affective) and acknowledge the accumulation of small steps of progress

(Behavioral) and present a clear focus of mind (Cognitive). When these parts are lined up together, you are more likely to translate your intentions into choices that result in the desired outcome. The second insight is to favor commitment over affirmation. Although affirmation is important for emotional support and encouragement, it has its limits. Constantly affirming something seldom leads to lasting change. Successful people do not say over and over, "I am a powerful person." Instead, they ask, "What do I really want? Am I prepared to take the steps to get it?" When you make a commitment, fully, you develop a laser focus to achieve your goal. Imagine you've already caught the fish. Your attention is on reeling it in.

How do we translate that attention into productive action? How can we maintain forward momentum when past habits have caused excess starts and stops? In short, how can we balance flexibility and grit? We create these new practices when we embrace rather than fight or flee from inevitable disappointments. Embrace what scares you. Know what you really need to protect when you lose your footing. Have a quiet place to go to, both an external peaceful sanctuary and an internal place of stillness in your mind."

We recommend some form of meditation to prime the pump for deep change. Amishi Jha, a Professor of Psychology at the University of Miami, and researcher on the science of attention, has worked with soldiers, firefighters, athletes, students and healthcare and business professionals to develop mindfulness exercises to develop "peak mind." Her studies have shown that a "centering meditation" for as little as 12 minutes a day will redirect a wandering mind. Meditation formats vary. Find one that fits you. The format can be a stationary practice (sitting, standing, or lying down), or a set of postures (yoga, qigong), or a moving postures (tai chi). It can focus on your breath, a sound, or an object. The key is to include these three components as you build your practice: relaxation, mental imagery, and mindfulness. How you meditate is not as important as why you meditate. Give yourself permission to regularly go to a quiet place where you can wrestle with your demons.

Listening to Our Inner Quiet

Having a place to go and a time to recharge your batteries is essential to bouncing back after disappointment. We would be remiss if we didn't mention resilience in this chapter. Resilience, that capacity to adapt, is a kissing cousin to grit. What gives people the strength needed to process and overcome hardship and stubborn habits? Dr. Andrea Pennington wrote a recent bestseller, *Top Ten Traits of Highly Resilient People.* One of the traits to build a stress-resilient personality is self-awareness. Resilient people are aware of situations around them, their own emotional reactions, and the behavior of those around them. By remaining aware, they can maintain control of a situation and think of new ways to tackle problems.

With self-awareness comes insight, that bit of self-knowledge which propels you to challenge your habits and beliefs. Insight is a peek under the hood to see how to balance negative and positive beliefs. It begins with simply noticing positive or negative thoughts and asking yourself: Where is this thought coming from? What are the assumptions about those thoughts? That's the beginning of real change.

Truth be told, a genuine metamorphosis in your thinking will involve a dramatic transformation in consciousness. In physics, the spontaneous change through a nuclear process of one element into another is called a transformation. For example, think about the change of water from a solid (ice cube) to a liquid (fluid water) to a gas (steam). Remember, this change process does not happen without a transfer of energy. Likewise, your personal transformation will require a transfer of energy on your part. In our experience, the use of queries can be an excellent prompt to stimulate that transfer of energy. A transformative change of your values, beliefs and aspirations starts with questioning your assumptions about change. Reflect on what you can do, *right now*, to create your most viable path. Begin with first-order change, the low hanging fruit of slowing down. Then graduate to second-order change by building up new habits. Strive to balance the tensions of the old you and the emerging you. Use these queries as you transfer fresh energy into a new way of knowing. And, of course, be kind to yourself during the process of change.

Queries:

- What do I need to change to allow my commitment to blossom?
- What is it costing me if I do not continue to change?
- What is it costing others close to me if I do not continue to change?
- Am I empowering others or enabling others with my unproductive choices?
- What will it cost me one year from now if I don't make the shift? (What will it cost me 5 years from now?)
- What baby steps can I take right now to fulfill my desires?
- What are the benefits for me (and for others) with a shift to a new commitment?
- Does the shift to a new commitment bring me a happier life?

Dr. Wayne's Story

My mid-life crisis was brought on by a perfect storm of too much work, not enough play, and a whole lot of loneliness. The years leading to my fall were a whirlwind: working on my doctorate, teaching undergraduate classes on penury wages, straining to fulfill my parental obligations, and subsisting on a lifestyle high on caffeine and low on sleep. It's no wonder that my first marriage imploded. I thought, erroneously, that I would right the balance when I landed a tenure-line position at a respected university. Nope, the dangling knife of "publish or perish" expectations kept me on the academic treadmill 24/7. In my mind, I was not worried. I prided myself on having a lot of energy and a strong physical constitution. I could do anything I put my mind to. I could meet any challenge. Then ... BAM! The well-designed house of cards supporting my invincibility crumbled with a snap of the fingers.

My push-push lifestyle was acid to my immune system. I was totally unprepared for the knockout punch. The fatigue, which I attributed to overwork and the effects of a lingering cold, were, in fact, symptoms of Crohn's Disease, an extremely painful inflammation of the digestive tract. My body collapsed. I couldn't eat solid foods. My well-planned life was in shambles. And my magnificent willpower, which had saved me from previous calamities, went AWOL. The old formulas of success no longer worked. I lost a third of my body weight. I lost one hundred percent of my confidence. I was desperate enough to pray. And that prayer was utterly simple: God, show me the way to good health. Happily, I was shown a way: seven abdominal surgeries in five years, a complete remake of my diet, daily meditation with a new mantra: focus on gratitude, not judgment. The necessary changes did not come easily. I am a stubborn guy. I yearned for the comforts of my old life. They never came. What did come, however, was the bounty of my present life. I set new goals. I failed. I learned from my mistakes and kept on steppin.' Grit matters.

Dr. Barb's Story

Pursuing a doctorate most certainly qualifies as an extreme sport. There are research classes to take, a Comp Exam to survive (the mother of all tests on everything you know), and, of course, that little project called the dissertation. It was such a roller coaster of emotions. One moment, I was excited and energized about advancing knowledge. However, that mood quickly dissipated when I tried to write in a scholarly fashion following accepted research protocols. No, no, there were way too many moving parts! And how does one share such a complicated project with family or friends? To help me get clarity about my topic my committee chair schooled me on the "elevator speech." It goes like this: a colleague you haven't seen in ages gets on the elevator, sees you and asks, "How's your research going? What's your dissertation about?" You have only enough time—two or three floors, at best—to unravel your spiel. Sheesh. My first thought was, "That certainly seems impossible."

Writing standards for a dissertation are exacting. The writing standards are exacting. One needs to be clear, precise, and concise and, for me, this does not qualify as natural behavior. Critical thinking and creativity have to be woven throughout each of the chapters. And the reward for my labors? I get an opportunity to "defend" my dissertation, a two-hour presentation followed by an extensive grilling by my committee. Invariably they asked a few questions (it seemed like a gazillion) that totally stumped me. So much for being the expert! After I passed (survived is more like it), I could reflect. What did the process teach me? My answer: you reach, then reach some more, then just when you think you are done reaching, you have to reach a bit further still.

Each dissertation is unique, but every grad student has a tale of an unexpected disaster, an incident that is beyond the pale. For me it involved a last second switcharoo. After I defended my dissertation, revised it, and hired a copy editor to dot i's and cross the t's to make it scholarship worthy, I turned in my precious document in to the Dean. The Dean initially signed off but then reconsidered. More "reach" was needed. This side trajectory blindsided me and my committee. What followed was an academic circus to get everyone on the same page. You've no doubt, heard the expression "politics which can play so rough." To say I was a stressed-out crazy woman doesn't even come close to what was actually going on in my head. Did I feel like giving up? Are you kidding? Every day! But something inside me, an insistent voice, kept up this mantra: "I earned this. I've worked hard for this. I will prevail." Throughout the entire process, my team stood by me; their grit was palpable. Finally, after oh-so-many revisions and tears, the masterpiece was deemed acceptable, and I got that coveted signature. Whew! A weight lifted off my shoulders. I was SO tired, but I had realized my goal. Grit matters.

Application Activities

Grit: Persistence in Spite of the Obstacles

1. Two Greek words connote different notions of time. *Kronos* time refers to chronological or sequential time, as in "I have a doctor's appointment at 2:00 pm." *Kairos* time signifies a time lapse, a moment of indeterminate time in which everything happens; the right or opportune moment (the supreme moment), as in "I was working on my stamp collection and totally lost track of time."

   Describe a situation where you were operating in *Kairos* time. What made this time special? Did your activity tap strong passion within you? How did you feel?

2. Rate yourself on these grit attributes. Circle the most accurate descriptor to these questions:

    a. Do you believe that effort beats talent?

      Always/most of the time/sometimes/never

    b. Do you believe that deliberate practice can increase resilience?

      Always/most of the time/sometimes/never

    c. Do you believe that grit is a learnable skill?

      Always/most of the time/sometimes/never

    d. Do you believe that moving from "commandment" mentality (victim thinking) to "commitment" mindset (creative thinking) can release restrictive beliefs?

      Always/most of the time/sometimes/never

    e. In dealing with failure or rejection when you fall down, can you accept "what is," rather than the story you tell yourself by which you interpret your circumstance?

      Always/most of the time/sometimes/never

    f. Can you be kind to yourself during the process of change?

      Always/most of the time/sometimes/never

3. The law of attraction is a belief that the magnetic power of the Universe draws similar energies together. It manifests through the power of creation. The premise of this law asserts that given an attitude

of gratitude and a clarity of intention, positive thoughts bring positive experiences into a person's life (and, equally, without a sense of gratitude and a consistent focus of intention, negative thoughts bring negative experiences into a person's life). It is the law and power that brings together people of similar interests, who unite into various groups, such as political groups, sports teams, sports fans, fraternities, etc.

a. How much do you identify with this belief? Circle the most accurate descriptor to this question:

Do I believe in the Law of Attraction?

Always/most of the time/sometimes/never

b. If you are open to broadening your belief that positive thoughts are magnets for positive life experiences, there are several things you can do. You can take advantage of this law through creative visualization and affirmations. By visualizing a mental image of what you want to achieve or by repeating positive statements, called affirmations, you create and bring into your life what you visualize or repeat in your mind. In other words, you use the power of your mind, thoughts, imagination, and words to help fulfill specific desires.

❖ Bring to mind your problem (see chapter 1, application number 1). Jot down two images of creative visualization that will help you focus joyfully on that desire:

❖ Bring to mind your problem (see chapter 1, application number 1). Jot down two affirmations that will help you focus joyfully on that desire:

4. Describe a time in your own life when you used grit to reach a goal. Was that situation unique or familiar? When you reflect upon it, was this an easy reach for the goal or did you really have to dig deep, and if so, how did you do that?

5. To avoid extreme peaks or valleys which can paralyze action, the authors of *Claim Your Life* advocate a "both/and" approach to problem solving. Therefore, "change" is paired with its opposite, "stability." Use a "both/and" response to a current unresolved problem

   a. Describe in a few words the nature of your unresolved problem (for example: relationship issue, money issue, health issue, etc.):

   b. Now provide some details to your Stability/Change response:

   STABLE - What will probably happen if I do not allow change?

   CHANGE - What will probably happen if I allow a change?

CHAPTER FOUR

Growth Mindset:
Facing Challenges by Learning
from Our Mistakes

"When people are ready to, they change. They never do it before then, and sometimes they die before they get around to it. You can't make them change if they don't want to, just like when they do want to, you can't stop them."

—Andy Warhol

"That he not busy being born is busy dying."

—Bob Dylan

My [WB] first real job after college was teaching in an inner-city elementary school. My students were categorized as low-income: they lived in a federal housing project surrounding the school; over 90% were on free or reduced lunches. Most kids came from single-parent homes.

Full-time work was scarce. The two nearby employers, a distillery, and a rendering plant, paid decent wages but offered no real job security; national companies were offshoring manufacturing jobs to cut labor costs. Families were transient, constantly on the lookout for cheap or safe housing. It was not out of the ordinary to see the same student on my class roster three separate times in a school year. During the warm months, the scent of marijuana drifted into our classroom window as teenagers openly smoked joints on the asphalt playground which doubled as a public park. Several of my students, even as early as second grade, were victims of random violence.

My colleagues and I experienced an impossibly huge disconnect between what was being taught in our teacher preparation classes as appropriate learning strategies and the chaos in my students' homes and neighborhood. My professional goal was to create lessons to help them thrive. However, their main focus was simply to survive. Nevertheless, by the end of my two-year Teacher Corps commitment, I realized how much we needed each other. From me, they learned how to think critically, engage collaboratively and respect diverse opinions and beliefs. From them, I learned that real learning wasn't going to happen unless it was relevant to their life, and it was fun.

Schools track academic progress through annual standardized testing. Ideally, the school's adequate yearly progress, or AYP, of a student, would be one year of academic gain in a nine-month school year. My incoming fourth graders should have been at the 3.9 or 4.0 level when we started the school year. However, my students' average reading score was 2.6; their math score was even lower, 1.9. That meant they were a year-and-a-half behind in reading and two years behind in math from their grade peers according to national averages...and they were only a quarter of the way through their 12-years of formal schooling. Expectations were low. My principal told us to aim at reducing annual academic loss by half (i.e., they would lose only 2–3 months per year rather than 5 in reading and 3-4 months rather than 7 in math). My students' parents were more practical, "Just keep them out of trouble and keep them in school. I can't afford to take off work for any foolishness."

Yet my expectations (and those of my Teacher Corps buddies) were far higher. If given the right resources and support, why couldn't they make a full year's progress in one academic year? That was our charge. We did all sorts of wild and crazy interventions, from experimenting with new instructional strategies (like small group discussion groups) to conducting "real world" research out in the community (like price comparisons for bread and milk from the same grocery chain, one a suburban store and the other an inner-city store). At first our students were mistrustful of our motives, but they eventually came to see that they could "own" their learning. School had become meaningful for them. Their academic scores skyrocketed. If they followed the pace from previous years, the end-of-the-year reading scores would have advanced from 2.6 to 3.1; the principal was shooting for a range of 3.3 or 3.4; I was hoping their average score would be 3.6. My kids' test scores surprised even me: They jumped from 2.6 to 4.1, a year-and-a-half academic gain in nine months... and from a rookie teacher at that. What did I do to make this happen? I got them to believe that they were smarter than they thought they were and that they could accomplish the things they value. In short, I got them motivated to move from fixed mindset to growth mindset.

The WHAT of Growth Mindset

Why do some kids succeed in school and others fail, even when they come from the same neighborhood or home? Educational policy and practice to close the achievement gap between low-and high-income students during the past 25 years has been a total bust. Again, why? The takeaway from the last chapter was this: we need grit to get past hard-to-give-up habits. Yet according to Camille A. Farrington, a former inner-city high school teacher who works at the University of Chicago Consortium on School Research, "There is little evidence that working directly on changing students' grit or perseverance would be an effective lever for improving their academic performance. While some students are more likely to persist in tasks or exhibit self-discipline in others, all students are more likely to demonstrate perseverance if the school or classroom context helps them develop positive mindsets and effective learning strategies." Her team discovered that a student's academic perseverance–how they maintained positive academic performance despite setbacks–depends on his or her academic mindset. Those students with a positive academic mindset had more resilience based on four key beliefs:

1. I belong in this academic community.
2. My ability and competence grow with my effort.
3. I succeed at this.
4. This work has value for me.

Students holding these beliefs in mind were more likely to persist through challenging academic work and not give up when their initial efforts failed. What explains this?

Two decades of research by Carol S. Dweck, a Professor of Psychology at Stanford University, has shown the enormous impact teachers have on a student's mindset. Her studies distinguish between two categories of behavior based on a student's reaction to failure, a fixed mindset, or a growth mindset. Professor Dweck claims that those with a fixed mindset believe that intelligence is static and impervious to change. That said, a student's best bet would be to look smart and avoid challenges which might endanger that image. When obstacles occur, they give up easily; effort is seen as fruitless. Therefore, they ignore useful feedback when it's perceived as negative and generally feel threatened by the success of others. As a result, they may plateau early and achieve less than their full potential, confirming their deterministic view of the world. On the other hand, students with a growth mindset believe that intelligence can be developed which leads to a desire to embrace challenges so they can learn more. They see effort as a path to mastery and persist in the face of setbacks. Therefore, they learn from constructive criticism and find useful lessons and inspiration in the success of others. As a result, they reach higher levels of achievement which give them a greater sense of free will.

In multiple studies, Professor Dweck and her colleagues noted that alterations in mindset could be achieved through praising the effort which led to success. Effective praise was not general ("Great effort. You tried your best.") but specific and contextual ("A good first try. This is new information for you. Learning happens in stages. The point is to grow into the next step. What are you going to try next?"). Such focused praise impacts a student's motivation toward achievement by satisfying their internal and external need for success.

Professor Dweck's research of mindsets has been useful in designing intervention strategies with at-risk students. Something as simple as practicing process praise and nurturing higher expectations can shift negative stereotypes of underachievers. Individuals who believe their talents can be developed (through hard work, good learning strategies, and constructive input from others) have a growth mindset. They tend to achieve more than those with a more fixed mindset (those who believe their talents are innate gifts). This is because they worry less about looking smart and they put more energy into learning.

Growth mindset is rapidly becoming a touchstone in business too. The terms change but the concepts remain: productive (or abundance) mindset versus the defensive (or scarcity) mindset. The productive mindset creates conditions for informed choices. Reasoning through a problem is viewed as a transparent process seen through different levels of an organization (ex: engineering, marketing, etc.). This encourages sustained effort for all departments to agree on new knowledge that can be verified. The defensive mindset, on the other hand, can be self-deceptive. When this mindset is active, people or organizations only seek out information that will protect them (or their departments). Truth can be shut out when it is seen as threatening. When entire companies embrace a growth mindset, their employees report feeling far more empowered and committed. They also receive far greater organizational support for collaboration and innovation. In contrast, people at primarily fixed-mindset companies report more cheating and deception among employees, presumably to gain an advantage in the talent race.

This illustrates the key difference between the two mindsets. Those with a fixed mindset focus on their perceived superiority, showing others that they are a somebody, not a nobody. Those with a growth mindset focus on their personal growth to achieve a success. One of the most profound applications of this insight has less to do with education or business, but with love. Professor Dweck found that people exhibited the same reactions in their personal relationships. Those with a fixed mindset believe their ideal mate would put them on a pedestal and make them feel perfect, whereas those with a growth mindset preferred a partner who would recognize their faults and lovingly help them become a better person. In the fixed mindset, the ideal is effortless and perpetual compatibility; cue to the end of a romantic movie: as the credits roll on the screen the implication is that the couple "lives happily ever." The growth mindset, however, says that you, your partner, and the relationship are capable of growth and change. The motivation in a growth-mindset relationship is to encourage your partner to learn new things and became a better person.

It's interesting to note how mindsets affect our response to disagreements. All relationships have conflict. When people with a fixed mindset talk about their conflicts, they assign blame. Sometimes they blame themselves, but more often they blame their partner. Making matters worse they claim that the responsibility for a fault or wrong is based on a personality trait, a character flaw. A predictable defensive reaction results. Since the problem comes from fixed traits, it can never be solved. So once people with the fixed mindset see flaws in their partners, they become angry and dissatisfied with the whole relationship. However, those with the growth mindset can acknowledge their partners' imperfections without assigning blame, and still feel that they have a fulfilling relationship. Conflicts are seen as problems of communication, not of personality or character. The irony is obvious. We begin a relationship with a partner who is different from us—it's the source of our attraction—and then become offended when those differences erupt in conflict.

In a healthy relationship people develop skills to deal with their differences. As they do, their relationship deepens. But for this to happen, people need to feel they're on the same side, the side of growth as an individual and growth as a couple. Success comes when effort is given to allow both my "me-ness" to grow and our "us-ness" to grow. A growth mindset says, "we'll get through this difficulty together." This unshakable validation of each other's development helps create an atmosphere of trust. Such trust sees setbacks as a heartening springboard for stretching existing abilities and connections. There is no perceived deficit. No need to prove a sense of worth. The focus is singular - just extend the effort to get better, individually, and together.

What it all comes down to is this: a mindset is an interpretative process that tells us what is going on around us. In a fixed mindset, that process is underscored by an internal monologue of constant judging and evaluation. Do I (or he, she, or they) measure up? However, in a growth mindset the internal monologue is not one of judgment but of curiosity. What input will lead to understanding and positive action?

The SO WHAT of Growth Mindset

Why is growth mindset such a hot topic right now? We get a hint from evolutionary psychology. This field attempts to explain mental and psychological attributes, such as memory, perception, or language as adaptations. Research in evolutionary psychology suggests that humans evolved social characteristics because group behavior helped them survive. Mindset studies can provide a context to explain human adaptation to changing environments. For example, we can ask: what is useful to produce more effective workplaces and classrooms? If employees or students believe their qualities were carved in stone—the fixed mindset—the prime motivation would be to look good and avoid taking personal responsibility for change. Someone with a fixed mindset focuses on looking smart and will not take on any challenge for fear of making mistakes or failing. Setbacks are not handled well since the fix mindseter perceives it as a threat to their intelligence. This can lead them to become defensive or discouraged and quit what they are working on. They will blame others for their own inability to complete a task and lie, and even cheat, to show themselves as smart and capable.

A growth mindset employee or student is not afraid of change. In this orientation the hand you are dealt is just the starting point for development. One question predominates: what can you cultivate through your efforts? Although people may differ in their talents, interests, or temperaments, there is a fundamental belief that everyone can change and grow through application and experience. The key for the employee or student is deliberate practice. The motivation for that practice was captured by the Bob Dylan quote at the beginning of the chapter, "That he not busy being born is busy dying." That act of being born, for growing anew, is both the carrot and the stick in facing a challenge. Persistence is rewarded. They believe their curiosity about new ideas and new ways of seeing a problem will help them solve future problems.

When a person with a growth mindset faces a new challenge, they take it on with the fascination of rising to a new level by expanding their repertoire of knowledge and skills. Three behaviors shine in growth-mindset individuals:

1. They are open to changing their mind when presented with compelling evidence. For example, in one study of a cognitive simulation which posed an anomaly or new information, growth-mindset people were more likely to change their initial understanding of a situation over previous beliefs.

2. They are hungry for feedback, positive or negative, as a means for growth. This frees them up considerably. They can risk making a mistake because they might find new strategies and behaviors to solve a problem.

3. They are more apt to use reflection as a way to gain fresh perspective. Unlike a fixed mindset person who sees reflection as extra effort, growth mindset people see reflection as part of the process of being a deliberate learner. However, a note of caution needs to be given. Eager to jump on this provocative bandwagon, many people jump to false conclusions about growth mindset. Professor Dweck identifies three common misconceptions

of a false growth mindset where the basic understanding of the idea is limited:

- Always had it, always will - People often confuse a growth mindset with having a positive outlook. Necessary but not sufficient. Growth is not a straight line; unexpected "surprises" cause us to zig and zag on the way to our goal. Actually, everyone is a mixture of fixed and growth mindsets, and that mixture continually evolves with experience. A "pure" growth mindset doesn't exist. We have to recognize that if we really want to grow.

- Praise matters more than outcomes—Nope. Hyperactive effort does not always ensure success. Even specific "process praise" may not be enough to reach your goals. Again, that quote by Einstein, "The definition of insanity is doing the same thing over and over again but expecting different results." Being mindful of what works and what doesn't work may be just as important as targeted praise.

- Talk the talk and good things will happen—Another nope. Slogans on the classroom wall or mission statements with lofty values about growth are not enough. Cultures supporting growth mindset recognize that walking the talk has short-term and long-term trajectories. Some risks won't work out. However, a short-term setback can be rewarded as a long-term learning opportunity.

Correcting these misconceptions may not guarantee reaching a growth mindset. We still have to deal with our own, often subconscious, fixed-mindset triggers. When we face challenges, receive criticism, or do poorly compared with others, we can easily fall prey to insecurity or defensiveness, a response that inhibits growth. Also, we need to recognize institutional barriers to a growth mindset. The classroom or office can be full of fixed-mindset triggers that impede growth such as a willingness to share information, collaborate, innovate, seek feedback, or admit errors. To remain in a growth zone, we must identify and work with these triggers. It takes courage to put growth mindset processes into practice. What constructive thoughts, words and behaviors will you use when confronted with a fixed-mindset demon? What can we do to model these practices toward a deeper, more engaged growth mindset?

The NOW WHAT of Growth Mindset

Growth mindset can be developed if given the proper guidance. Attitude and perspective about a new task make all the difference in the world. A teacher who can present something challenging as fun and exciting will have a better chance at nurturing the growth mindset. A boss who practices servant leadership by recognizing teamwork or spotlighting mentors who reinforce best practices with new staff will have a better chance of creating growth mindset in the workplace. The trick, of course, is managing expectations. Some stress is helpful; it can focus attention. Too much stress is distracting or debilitating; it can lead to self-doubt. Understanding the opportunities and threats in allowing an employee or a student to struggle (and even falter on a low-stakes task) can motivate them to recover from failures. Learning flexible and effective problem-solving and self-care strategies can improve self-confidence and team trust.

However, Professor Dweck and her colleagues are finding an unsettling disconnect between the talk and walk of growth mindset. During workshops and presentations around the country she hears stories from many teachers and parents who endorse growth mindset rhetoric, but react to children's mistakes in ways that unintentionally promote fixed mindset practice. For example, reiterating the message "just try harder" can backfire. Most students have heard "just try harder," ad nauseam. They also need to understand why they should put in effort and how to deploy that effort. Compare these two statements:

1. "Don't worry, you'll get it if you keep trying."
2. "That problem is hard. I've seen you do hard things before. Remember what you did then that'll help you solve this problem."

The first statement is feel-good cheerleading. The second statement uses the student's past success as evidence to bolster his or her current effort. Responding with growth mindset thinking will require us to relearn how we deal with challenges. Professor Dweck's remedy is to match the words and actions of growth mindset with our fixed-mindset triggers. Here is what she has to say:

> Watch for a fixed-mindset reaction when you face challenges. Do you feel overly anxious, or does a voice in your head warn you away? Watch for it when you face a setback in your teaching, or when students aren't listening or learning. Do you feel incompetent or defeated? Do you look for an excuse? Watch to see whether criticism brings out your fixed mindset. Do you become defensive, angry, or crushed instead of interested in learning from the feedback? If you are a business manager watch what happens when you see a colleague who's better than you at something you value. Do you feel envious and threatened, or do you feel eager to learn? Accept those thoughts and feelings and work with and through them. (Dweck, Ph.D. Carol S., *Mindset: The New Psychology of Success*, Ballentine Books, 2007)

It takes a lot of work and a lot of time for this reorientation to feel natural. We must avoid the temptation to oversimplify, for example: growth mindset means you are an enlightened person and fixed mindset means you are an unenlightened person. We have seen teachers and office workers immediately claim a growth mindset identity after just one workshop. How can we break through this limiting mindset thinking? Again, Professor Dweck to the rescue. She urges us to use dual voice (both/and) responses. We're all a mixture of fixed and growth mindsets. The key is to practice, again and again, these essential growth mindset principles:

- Intelligence can be developed
- The brain is malleable
- Doing challenging work is the best way to make the brain stronger and smarter

If we watch carefully for our fixed-mindset triggers, we can begin the true journey to a growth mindset.

Mindsets can be changed, but most American schools don't do a good job of creating environments to develop growth mindset and effective learning strategies. Some teachers have been able to create such an environment in their own classroom regardless of the school climate; however school-wide strategies promoting growth mindset have been rare. Paul Tough, the author of the best-selling book, *How Children Succeed*, has documented several schools that help students become more resilient. Turnaround for Children (https://turnaroundusa.org) is a nonprofit school transformation network, with schools in New York, Newark, New Jersey, and Washington, DC. They coach teachers to provide a more inviting emotional atmosphere by creating a climate of belonging and engagement in the classroom. Students can follow the muse of their curiosity when a variety of instructional strategies are employed, such as cooperative learning, small group peer review, and collaborative long-term projects. The EL (Expeditionary Learning) Education, a national nonprofit network of 150 schools throughout the country, has a particular emphasis on high poverty schools. EL education successfully uses two strategies to develop an ongoing academic mindset with its students. The first strategy deals with belonging and relationship and the second immerses students in challenging academic work. Classrooms are designed to be more engaging and interactive than classrooms in most American schools. Students feel more motivated when they experience deep and close relationships with teachers and peers and do work that is challenging, rigorous and meaningful.

However, such schools are rare. Teachers and parents who are drawn to such empowering environments of education can find comprehensive strategies through the online Khan Academy growth mindset lesson plan.

Here's a sample of the type of activities in their plan:

- As a teacher, share a personal story about a time you had to work hard to get better at something and relate it to the video. In this story, highlight:
  1. Hard work
  2. Strategies
  3. Help from others

- Ask your students for a short story about a struggle they had when they were learning. How did it make them feel? How did they overcome it, and what did it teach them? Tell them to write a letter to a future student to tell them about their struggle, what they learned from it, and any advice they could give for the student

- Have students do a research project on how the brain grows as it struggles to learn something new. Ask students to create a poster, diorama, video, or PowerPoint presentation to showcase how the brain works. Also be sure that students include evidence to back up their claims. Encourage students to be creative and scientific when explaining how learning can help develop the brain.

For example, 'what is neuroplasticity and how does it work?

- What are neurons? How can they change over time? How do we know this?
- What are ways of making your brain grow?
- What is a growth mindset?

The consequences of believing that intelligence can be developed has profound implications. With growth mindset you know you can change over time. This allows you to reflect, learn and grow when the going gets tough. Love of learning replaces fear of failure as you face a looming challenge. What internal changes can polish your lens to see potential obstacles as opportunities? A good place to start is to pay attention to your inner quiet.

Listening to Our Inner Quiet

A growth mindset is expansive and deeply connected to a sense of awe and wonder. William Blake captures this sensibility by reminding us to "kiss the joy as it flies." When we are consciously connected to creating the reality of our dreams, a feeling of appreciation naturally arises. It makes sense. Why wouldn't we be thankful after we give ourselves permission to let our heart's desire open us up? A growth mindset increases in proportion to our ability to see what's good in life. This potential gets fed when we exhibit an attitude of gratefulness. By not taking life for granted we become curious for everything life offers, even with disruptions that come up unexpectedly.

When we can be more open and accepting of whatever feeling is on our plate, gratitude blossoms naturally. The 20th century German poet, Rainer Maria Rilke, understood this fluidity of life, "Let everything happen to you. Beauty and terror. Just keep going. No feeling is final." Now take a step back and personalize this attitude. Think of a time in your life when you showed sincere appreciation for the "beauty and terror" of your fate. Perhaps it was a threatening situation that needed to be assimilated. Perhaps it was a pushback on a robotic internal monologue which was eroding your self-worth. Use these queries to let the light of gratitude shine on the shadows surrounding unfinished business in your life. Give yourself permission to count your blessings.

- What do I take for granted?
- What relationships in my life do I cherish (with people, pets, etc.)?
- What unique gifts or opportunities do I have?
- What advantages or freedoms have I been given in life?
- Who is my support crew, the champions in my life?

Finally, meditate on this snippet by Joseph Campbell, who brought fresh wisdom to old myths: "The demon that you can swallow gives you its power, and the greater life's pain, the greater life's reply."

Dr. Wayne's Story

This may seem frivolous but my change from fixed mindset to growth mindset involved dancing with my wife. Actually, it's more basic than that. I was terrified about being on a dance floor. I knew, without hesitation, that everybody was looking only at me and was wincing at my uncoordinated gyrations. Although I felt good about my body image and enjoyed playing several sports, when it came to cutting the rug I was a hot mess. I did my due diligence in trying to learn new dance moves (in the privacy of my home, of course). I studied film, mostly of Fred Astaire and Gene Kelly. I imagined I was a gazelle. But, in reality, I knew who I was—a heavy hippo. As fate would have it, I married a woman who really loved to dance. Her movements were quite graceful, too. She simply glided around the dance floor as if she was an Olympic ice skater. When we were courting, she tried everything to get me to move rhythmically. "Just relax," she'd coo, "and let your body follow the beat of music." I heard her words, but they did not compute physically. My body felt like a brick. I was a hopeless case.

That changed the day she accidentally unlocked the combination to my winged feet. The timing and setting were so unexpected. We were packing for a move. Boxes, some packed, most not, cluttered our living room. We were hot and tired. One of our favorite songs came on the radio. She took my hand and spontaneously spun me around in a little pirouette. I have no memory what happened after that. We swayed, we whirled, we twirled. The song ended but we continued to dance. Finally, we collapsed in a heap on the couch. She shook her head from side to side and asked, "What just happened?" I shrugged my shoulders and said, "I dunno, but that was fun, wasn't it?" Truth be told, I dropped my need to hide behind my perceived deficiency and just let the passion of the moment carry me away. That moment was a real deal changer. I realized I could put new wine in old skins. I wanted to recreate this moment again. Happily, my wife and I have had numerous opportunities for "deliberate practice." I know I am not the most elegant guy on the dance floor, but I have fun stretching myself and now look forward to dancing. Growth mindset matters.

Dr. Barb's Story

Sometimes new ways of thinking come out of unexpected places. Making life decisions has always been challenging for me. I am the type of person who has to know all of the options and then I think through each of the details—the implications, consequences, and fantasies—of why one choice is better than another. And, heaven forbid, I don't let anyone know how much obsessing I do! It's an exhausting process. Sometimes this constant self-questioning simply paralyzes me.

For instance, a while back, a coveted job offer, complete with two separate trainings, was dumped in my lap. Naturally, I was excited...until I saw the dates of the trainings. The multi-day trainings came at the same time as a dear friend's wedding and another "must do" event which had been scheduled seven months earlier. What to do?

What to do? Before, I would have fretted privately. This time I did something new. I called up a friend and fretted with him. I talked and talked and talked about the implications, consequences, and fantasies of the decision until I had nothing left to say. At the end of our conversation, two things became apparent to me: the decision needed to come more from my heart than my head and speaking my truth was really, really important. When I truly listened to myself, I "knew" that my heart was at peace. I had a resolution: I would be available for the first training, and I would need to miss the second training. I notified the firm. The ball regarding next steps was now in their court. I felt relieved and would accept whatever outcome happened.

Indeed, this was a growth mindset for me. My natural inclination was a fixed response, to please others first before attending to my own needs. Having that conversation with a friend when I was most vulnerable was a huge step for me. I was able to compare two different assessments of the situation and I was affirmed for sharing the rumblings of my heart. Growth mindset matters.

Application Activities

Growth Mindset: Facing Challenges by Learning from Our Mistakes

1. A Fixed Mindset (FM) is a belief that intelligence is set for life. Therefore, all effort is geared to upholding an image of being smart or looking good. When obstacles occur, any negative feedback is seen as threatening. This results in achieving less, giving up easily and adopting a fatalistic view of life.

    A Growth Mindset (GM) is a belief that intelligence is fluid and can be developed. Effort is seen as the key to mastery and persistence. In the face of setbacks, you can grow your problem-solving skills, curiosity and confidence through hard work, good strategies, and input from others.

In the blank before each of the following descriptions, write FM if the behavior or belief represents a Fixed Mindset or GM if the behavior or belief represents a Growth Mindset. *

a. _____ It's a dog-eat-dog world. If I don't protect myself, who will?

b. _____ When in doubt, it's important to show a sign of strength.

c. _____ Talent can be developed through effort and seeking help from others.

d. _____ Working your hardest means establishing your superiority.

e. _____ Working your hardest means doing and becoming your best.

f. _____ In a conflict, point out the obstacles created by the other person.

g. _____ In a conflict, the problem comes from fixed traits, it can't be solved.

h. _____ In a conflict, acknowledge one's partners imperfections without assigning blame.

i. _____ In a conflict, the problem is of communication, not personality or character.

j. _____ Success comes through effort, feedback and seeking assistance from others.

2. Think of a past success in which you reached a particular goal or milestone in your life. Give a short answer response to each question below:

    a. Describe the goal or milestone.

    b. What caused you to persevere?

    c. Did your skill or confidence grow by your effort?

    d. What surprised you? For example, what sustained you when others doubted your persistence?

3. Think of a mistake you made recently. What were your thoughts or feelings before others became aware of what happened? What did you do after the mistake became known?

    a. Describe a situation where you used feedback, both positive and negative, in a productive way?

    b. Describe a situation where you used feedback, either positive or negative, in an unproductive way?

    c. Compare these two stories. How might you use feedback as a means for growth? How can making a mistake help you find new strategies and behaviors to solve a problem?

4. Compare these two praise statements. Which do you think would be more effective to instill long-lasting change? Why?

    - "Great effort. You tried your best."

    - "A good first try. This is new information for you. How can you use it for the next step?"

5. Share a personal story about a time you had to work hard to get better at something. In this struggle story include specific examples of:

- Hard work
- Strategies to overcome obstacles
- Seeking help from others.

* Answers for number 1: GM for c, e, h, i, j

CHAPTER FIVE

Living With Our Questions

"Live your questions now, and perhaps even without knowing it, you will live along some distant day into your answers."

—Rainer Maria Rilke

A thought exercise: Draw a horizontal line on a paper, 12 inches in length. Now extend the line 3 inches on each side with dotted lines. The right end of the line represents your fluid life, your abundant life, the life as you choose to live in the present moment from an I/Thou perspective. The left end of the line represents your fixed life with a focus on deficits and limitations, a life conditioned by expectations from others, fixated on the past or future. These are symptoms of an I/It perspective. The solid line is what you already know; the dotted lines are what's unknown, what experiences and people you are attracting. Now place a fulcrum somewhere along the solid horizontal line as a graphic representation of how you view your life unfolding. Be as honest and nonjudgmental as you can. If the fulcrum is not at the midpoint of the horizontal line (a rare event for most of us) and you are eager to find a rough balance, pay attention to the dotted lines. The fulcrum is a stationary point. The weight and length of the line are the variables you can control to find balance.

An image from my childhood tells the tale. As a teenager, I remember holding my five-year-old sister hostage in the up position by sitting down on my end of the see-saw. If she had more weight on her side or if I moved closer to the center (or a combination of the two), the teeter-totter would be in perfect balance. Same with your needs and aspirations as you strive to live into your fullness. What are you going to move (surrender) on the left side of the line or give weight to (intentionality) on the right side of the line to find a rough balance? What questions do you need to ask yourself to move toward that balance?

This chapter is about applying your combination of the Key 3 (empathy, grit, or growth mindset) to your particular hot-button issue. It asks the question: How do I claim my light to get unstuck from negative beliefs and follow my calling? First though, a digression on the art of questioning. Effective questioning is the lifeblood of a teacher, a counselor, or a mediator. Questioning taps into the art of learning. It is WAY more important than spitting out a "correct" answer. And despite what your teachers may have told you, there is such a thing as a bad question. A bad question forces a learner to get into the mind of the teacher and summon a superficial answer. This response to a question focuses on pleasing the question-asker; factual recall is the reward (ex: In 1492, who sailed the ocean blue?). This type of question represents lower order thinking. A good question, on the other hand, forces the learner to make a deep dive into his or her mind. The response to a good question encourages independent and original thinking; students are rewarded for curiosity and risk-taking (ex: What kind of supplies would Columbus need for his voyage, especially if he didn't know how long it would take?). This type of question represents higher order thinking. Answering a challenging question takes into account the context of the situation (the complexity of the circumstance) and the competing perceptions of possible answers.

Which brings us back to you. In the first chapter we proposed an educational model to help make your dreams come true. We suggested the Key 3 principles—empathy, grit, and growth mindset—to reframe the story of who you say you are. In this chapter we get personal. Consider these questions:

- Are you willing to ask yourself the tough questions to increase your learning capacity?

- Are you willing (at least in your mind's eye) to be open-minded and open-hearted on the journey to become a more competent and confident you?

- Finally, are you willing to be more accountable in making and maintaining sustainable changes, even after you initially fall down?

If you answered "yes," then you are ready to live your questions now. Use the questions posed in this chapter as a touchstone to grapple with your issue whether it's overcoming negativity to change an unproductive behavior or belief, or dissolving the barriers to your calling. Will you trust your instincts to follow new hunches? Our caveat: as ludicrous as it sounds, embrace these questions as much as you can, especially the scary ones.

The WHAT of questioning

Effective questions are questions that are thought-provoking. The most effective questions are less concerned with an immediate (and often superficial) answer but in what new questions it raises. They are not "why" questions, but "what" and "how" questions. "Why" questions can lead us to reinforce set beliefs instead of disrupting set beliefs. Rather than soliciting a fresh point of view, "why" questions can scratch insecurities and make people defensive. Instead, ask more powerful questions about what's going on and how conditions might be changed.

Effective questions linger. The kind of questions we ask expose what we're really after, lower-order thinking or higher-order thinking. We can ask closed questions or open questions. Closed questions give a narrow focus and can be helpful when checking facts, clarifying a point, or providing some direction on the topic at hand. These are usually beginning questions that give boundaries to an issue. Open questions provide more breadth and depth and can be helpful for gaining more detailed information, exploring ideas, and clarifying thoughts. These are usually the follow-up questions that give context to an issue. Consider some of these questions as you work with your particular issue. Frame your issue as a question. Start with easy questions and progress to more challenging ones.

- What causes me to abandon my effort after a disappointment (ex: losing weight, eating right, exercising, making more money, finding a right-fit job, finding a compatible partner, etc.)?
- How does this situation mirror an aspect of myself?
- What are my old mental messages or beliefs about this?
- What tools can help me reframe this situation?

Effective questions follow effective listening. When asking effective questions, it is important to listen mindfully to get to a deeper level of understanding. Listening in this manner allows the student or client to come up with their own solution or plan of action.

We use the information we find from careful listening to ask more effective questions. Notice the progression of your questioning. Your questions may move from a simple to a more complex sequence, from describing ("What I hear you saying is ...") to clarifying ("Here's what I hear you say-ing. Is that right?) to being curious ("What's motivating you to do this?"). Finally, allow enough silence between finish-ing a question and getting an answer for a more complete response to bubble up. Classroom teachers are advised to practice the "four-second wait rule" before responding to a question. This gives the student enough time to form a more authentic reply. Seasoned questioners watch the eyes and nonverbals of students processing the question; it usually takes a moment for the proverbial lightbulb to turn on.

These examples of effective questioning and listening assume a mutual communication loop: Am I being heard? Do I feel comfortable risking an out-of-box question? Is the discussion interesting and engaging? We have also found that this process can be used as a solo practice between your past self and your emerging self. For example:

- What feelings came up after I unintentionally broke my diet? (describing)
- Do I have a Plan B in place to cover this situation? If not, what would it look like? (clarifying)
- What unmet need toppled my intent? (furthering curiosity)

Effective questions prompt new possibilities. A well-crafted question invites one to consider new perspectives or inter-pretations of unexplored turf. Just asking, "What's the connection between 'this or that' expands awareness of a situation which can prompt multiple layers of meaning." Powerful questions can help us suspend judgment, thereby allowing the good stuff to bubble up.

The SO WHAT of questioning

Effective questioning of our change process is a bit like the one-shoe-dropping phenomenon. As we wait for the other shoe to drop, we are alert to what's coming next. The "So What?" of questioning involves paying closer attention to our own accountability. Not judging our efforts, mind you, but gathering data to allow us to make better decisions. This is where we get a peek to how our aliveness can shine. Mahatma Gandhi got to the nut of this matter when he wrote, "As human beings, our greatness lies not so much in being able to remake the world, but in being able to remake ourselves." That said, let's explore two questions on the journey of remaking ourselves. They get at the impediments to realizing our greatness:

- How can I undo the priority I give to self-judgment?

Many people believe that those who are successful are free from self-doubt and insecurities. Not true. We've worked with many students and clients who belie their achievements and reputations with negative, often brutal, self-talk. The huge disconnect between their outer success and their inner negative feelings about themselves leads to a paralysis. They seem unable to accept changes that would lead to a greater peace of mind. We recognize that we can't avoid negative self-judgments. All we ask is: Can you release the death grip of expectations ever so slightly? Can you apply a "both/and" perspective to your situation? What would that look like? Judgment can be both helpful and not helpful. Helpful: judgments that are akin to discernment, our first-line protection against rejection or failure. Our internal dialogue gives us a running account of perceived threats. Not helpful: too much judgment can get in the way of solving problems, hurt other people's feelings when you didn't mean to, or harm your own self-esteem and happiness. So, what's the Rx for finding a "both/and" balance?

The way out of this predicament is to dive directly into the mess headfirst with a curiosity to discern what you can and cannot control. First become aware of the feelings behind the judgment (e.g., fear, anxiety, anger, depression, guilt, etc.) and then ask yourself, "Is the narrative behind the feelings 100% true or just a story I am telling myself?" If it is not 100% true, then tap into your inner wisdom and ask, "What is the real truth here?" If you are sincerely open to genuine change, the truth will inadvertently pop into your mind, and it will be much different from the story you've been telling yourself. Following this path makes it easier to let go of resistance and tune in to your deeper passion and move forward with confidence.

We have found two useful ways to foster this sense of self-encouragement. First, disable your self-accuser.

Recognize your imperfections and respond with a dose of unconditional love. Use the power of silliness to defuse emotional triggers and reduce your need to diminish yourself or others. Reframe heavy seriousness with light-hearted absurdity. For example, you might replace, "I am so controlling, and I can't live with myself" with "My control mania looks like slapstick comedy. How hilarious!" Taking away the heaviness of the self-criticism makes it easier to embrace the healing powers of love. Eventually you'll have the courage to say, "I am controlling, *and* I am learning to live with myself." Second, vow not to be offended. Know how to sidestep the blame game. After moaning to a friend about an incident where I was treated wrong, a dear friend, remarked, "I get that. I've been called everything in the book. I've finally learned not to be offended." Incredulously, I asked, "How?" His reply was so simple, "I ask just one question, "Is it true?" If it is, I accept it and forgive myself. If I don't identify with it, then it's not my problem. It's the other guy's stuff?"

- How can I be happy despite my perceived deficits?

Developing I/Thou thinking is powerful but don't hold yourself to unrealistic standards and expect a quick transformation of lifelong habits. Although it's impossible to be totally free from self-judgment, you can alter the reception of what others say and learn from them. See this as a part of an ongoing mindfulness practice. Whenever a barbed criticism comes barreling into your mind, respond only by saying under your breath "thought." This neutral labeling immediately does two things: it deactivates the energetic sting of the criticism, and it allows you to return to the present moment. This eliminates the connection to the demons of your past or delusions of your future. Also, as much as possible, go beyond basic behavior change and allow your consciousness to expand accordingly. In *The Art of Happiness*, the Dalai Lama points the way of seeing yourself in a new light, "A disciplined mind leads to happiness, and an undisciplined mind leads to suffering. If you want others to be happy, practice compassion. If you want to be happy, practice compassion."

So, how can we practice compassion, for ourselves and for others, in our hurried, harried world? We offer four possibilities:

- Meditation

  Happiness is an inside job; practice quieting the mind. Whatever the form (ex: mantra, sitting meditation, tai chi) meditation takes away the distractions of the mind. Happiness is about being, not doing.

- Meaning

  Our lives matter. What gives purpose to our life comes from what we value. When we give ourselves, wholeheartedly, to others or a cause we are rewarded with a deep emotional satisfaction.

- Gratitude

  When we acknowledge the good, despite appearances, we become more thankful. Seeing the opportunities hidden in adversity reminds us that we have the gift of choice in how to respond to challenges.

- Generosity

  The more generous we are, the more we get back. For example, Alcoholic Anonymous sponsors are twice as likely to stay sober as non-sponsors. Sharing and giving makes us feel better. When we simply "think" of helping someone, our endorphins increase.

Finally, know that happiness is a byproduct of living well; don't chase after it. Continue developing a disciplined mind by asking essential questions to increase your consciousness and solidify the change you want to see.

The NOW WHAT of questioning

Claiming your light means being aware of your surroundings. That means recognizing your consciousness and how your mind interprets the world. David R. Hawkins M.D., Ph.D., a renowned psychiatrist, researcher, and spiritual teacher, had a succinct description about how shifting one's consciousness leads to change, "Consciousness advances when it's provided essential information, then activated by intention. This prompts inspiration, humility and surrender which lead to dedication and perseverance." We've tried to follow this formula as we designed this book. We provided essential information through the content of the Key 3: empathy, grit, and growth mindset. We hope the sections on "Listening to Our Inner Quiet" help you develop a stronger intent. We equally hope that the questioning strategies in this chapter prompt inspiration, humility, and surrender. Here are a few practical ideas to keep steadfast when dealing with obstacles along the way.

When trying out new life strategies, a good rule of thumb is the "one-step removed" guideline. It's easy to become resistant or distracted when dealing with a problem that has bedeviled you for years. However, given some distance, a knotty problem can look less frightening or confusing. That distance may be of time or person. Here's how the "one-step removed" rule works with time. Think of an embarrassing moment from your recent past that caused you to wince. Perhaps it was some slight that's still tender to your heart. Now think of an embarrassing moment from your distant past, maybe something that happened to you as a child or adolescent. Chances are that enough time has passed to heal that mortifying moment from long ago. Ask yourself what's changed over time to shrug off that uncomfortable encounter. What perceptions have shifted inside that allow you to laugh at something that once caused you to suffer? What attitude do you now have that immediately calms the trigger which provoked you long, long ago? This is your innate wisdom. It's the most updated version of yourself, reminding you that you can survive an embarrassing moment. Now take that wisdom, that new attitude about yourself, and apply it to the current embarrassment. See, you do have the tools to overcome a potentially negative response. You can break the vicious cycle of victimization.

Here's how the "one-step removed" rule works with any person. An alternate pathway to move from victim cycle to virtuous cycle is to think of someone you know who has successfully changed a habit you are now dealing with (like not becoming paralyzed when embarrassed). Go through the same process as you followed when applying wisdom from the past to a present problem. How does this success-ful someone inspire new behavior? How does this champion in your life model fresh attitudes and insights? The "one-step removed" rule is a way of asking questions of your earlier self or of someone else to help you take the necessary baby steps toward the new territory of sustainable change.

As you enter that new territory, be kind to yourself. Remember that simply wanting to change a belief is not always enough to make that change permanent. Beliefs are programmed deeply into the mind, and you have collected evidence for many years to support this view. If you have a setback about an intended goal or new belief, that just means you need to go deeper. Pay attention to perceived agreements inside your mind that support your story of how the world works. Going deeper means accessing your inner guide and knowing the difference between knowledge and wisdom. Knowledge is the information that has been put in your mind by others or by the culture and times in which you live. Wisdom transcends a life limited by an old belief system and opens the heart and mind to celebrate the beauty and wonder inherent in all life.

Trusting an instinct about your innate wisdom creates a personal freedom from limiting beliefs and agreements. To break free of the unconscious programming of limiting beliefs you must be willing to investigate adverse memories from the past, specifically the emotional charge attached to those memories. Two effective approaches to gain this freedom is through taking a personal inventory and recapitulation. The first step is to find a place of peace inside you, a place that feels safe. Then take an inventory of what triggered your fear, anger, or sadness. Revisit that discomfort from a perspective of "healing empowerment." Who were the heroes and villains in that memory? Get to the moment when you shut down, where your need to protect yourself was strongest.

This prepares you for recapitulation. From your current perspective of "healing empowerment," confront the discomfort in a healthy and useful manner. Follow this three-step breathing meditation: First, on the inhalation, imagine something hot, dark, and heavy; on the exhalation, imagine something white, light, and cool. Second, on the inhalation, imagine your adverse memory; on the exhalation, imagine a moment of joy. Third, on the inhalation, imagine someone else who has suffered the same fate; on the exhalation, imagine sending this person blessings of peace and happiness. Repeat the meditation until the electrical charge has diminished. Conscious recapitulation can cleanse long-held pain. From this bird's eye view of a decontaminating a past emotional wound, you begin the long process of becoming more responsive and resilient. This is the process of becoming a more vibrant and authentic person.

Listening to Our Inner Quiet

In sports, as in war, there is a defensive game and an offensive game, the former for protecting and the later for scoring. In business, a defensive strategy is designed to reduce the risk of loss, to protect your share of the market in order to keep your customers happy and your profits stable. On the other hand, an offensive competitive strategy pursues changes within an industry, usually with investments in technology and research and development, to be a trend-setter and stay ahead of the competition. Few excel at both. This analogy characterizes personal change. To claim your light, you can choose the carrot approach or the stick approach to fashion your new life. Will I send in the offensive team or the defensive team to gain insight for a fulfilling life? For example, you might employ a defensive strategy towards getting unstuck from negativity by asking yourself how you can adjust your personal drama, how you can reduce your loss and address unmet needs? An offensive plan might involve slipping past self-imposed barriers or breaking free and score big points to your deeper calling. That means seeing yourself as a trend-setter and following the charge made by Henry David Thoreau, "Go confidently in the direction of your dreams!

Live the life you've imagined." Here are some questions to live the life you've imagined:

- What happened today that made you keep going to satisfy unmet needs?
- What did you learn from that? What's your takeaway?
- What surprised you or what mistakes did you make that taught you something?
- What strategy are you going to try to get back on track?

Spoiler alert: Living your deepest truth will require you to give up a sizable chunk of your status quo. Not everything, mind you, just those areas which no longer fit who you are right now, the person you are becoming. Expect pushback from others, especially from those closest to you. They have grown comfortable with that well-worn older version of yourself. Your journey toward your dreams might very well challenge their complacency. It is tempting to fall back into the numb-inducing trance that has been the source of your suffering. Change doesn't come with any guarantees. It most certainly doesn't come with a playbook. Expect to encounter discomfort. And wonder. And surprises galore. So, remember the bottom line: you, and only you, are in charge of your life. Let your vision do the talking and be ready to adjust plans along the way. Marcel Proust had it right, "The real voyage of discovery consists not in seeking new landscapes, but in seeing with new eyes."

As he was approaching his own death, Dr. Stuart Farber, a palliative care physician at the University of Washington, reflected on patient care and what he referred to as his thread. "With rare exception, the clinicians who treated me have good hearts, care deeply, but possess little to no knowledge of my thread. My thread is the narrative I use to make sense of my life. It is longitudinal, non-linear, and emotional, filled with contradictions, and integrates my life experiences into a coherent whole. It is within the values and meanings of my story that treatment decisions are made. What contributes to meaning and quality is not about living longer but living a life that is consistent with my thread. Without knowing my thread, it is impossible for a clinician to provide respectful care." Indeed. That's the premise of this book, boiled down to 21 words: "What contributes to meaning and quality is not about living longer but living a life that is consistent with my thread." That's the insight that makes for a fulfilling life. So, what's your thread? What's your soul's hunger?

Dr. Wayne's Story

When I was in my late twenties and early thirties, I had a recurring dream which terrified me. In the dream I was a circus acrobat hanging forty feet above the ground. My job was straightforward: to let go of the handle of one swing, turn to my right 180 degrees and catch an approaching swing in midair. But I wondered, would the approaching swing really be in place when I needed to grab it? What if it came crashing into my body as I completed the turn or, worse yet, be just out of reach? Actually, I didn't just wonder…I obsessed over the different permutations of disaster that awaited me. It is said that dreams reflect unresolved issues in one's life. True that. This time was a hectic period in my life where I needed to master several huge unrelated tasks all at once—a new marriage, new kids, and a new job. My career aspirations were the most vexing. How could I possibly carve my own space as a teacher given the high standards set by my mother, an elementary school teacher, and by my father, a college professor? It felt like I was juggling too many balls in the air, and I couldn't afford to drop any one of them without dire consequences. No wonder I obsessed over my predicament. My anxiety increased with each passing dream. I turned in midair and froze, blind to my surroundings.

The dream seemed to show up when I had too many "must make" deadlines in my life. I needed to release this tension…like NOW. I finally hit the wall. Or, more precisely, I hit the floor. One night I was so physically wrapped up in the dream that I fell out of bed! There I sat, dazed, with a goofy grin on my face. "Oh yeah," I thought, "I can look up." This was followed by a rapid-fire awareness, "I can look up or down or to the right or left. I don't have to look just straight ahead." My emotional dam broke. I laughed and laughed until my sides hurt. There was more than one way to "see" when fear had its grip on me. I had options. It was like trying on a new pair of eyes. I chuckled to myself and got back into bed. Slept like a baby. That dream never returned.

Dr. Barb's Story

Have you ever felt invisible? Far too often in my personal and professional life I'd have to answer "yes." What makes it even worse is how often it was because of my own choices. Why did I stay in situations that were uncomfortable and left me feeling unfulfilled and empty? In one job I was low woman on the totem pole. My ideas were routinely disregarded, and my input was not valued by the team. I voiced my concern with the manager who told me that her view of the workplace was in line with the company's standards. She assumed I understood the culture of the company, even though this code was not verbalized. One day I had an aha moment. I was not there to meet their standards; I was there to be visible. My professional strength of connecting and building relationships with others was not valued in this particular job. I honestly don't even believe they knew what value I could bring to the table. I launched into being visible but that meant a change, I needed to find a place that valued what I valued.

Truth be told, I knew what I wanted. But finding my true path toward vulnerability, enlightenment, and depth of self has not been an easy route. I've had so many twists and turns and roadblocks along the way. The most vexing barrier was my need to listen to my truth and respect my own needs instead of only pleasing others. A huge weight was lifted when I left that job precisely because it did not feed my soul. An even larger weight was lifted when I released the negative people and dark energy that drained me of my zest for life. That's my focus now, to keep my zest in the forefront and live a life of opportunity, growth, and new possibilities. The journey is now well underway. I will continue to speak my truth as I know it and not knowingly allow myself to become invisible. I am finding my thread.

Application Activities
Living With Our Questions

1. What is one goal that I never seem to reach (ex: losing weight, finding satisfaction with my work, financial independence, relationship harmony, etc.)?

   YES   NO   a. Despite previous setbacks in reaching your goal, do you believe the Key 3 (empathy, grit, growth mindset) can help move you toward your goal?

   YES   NO   b. Are you willing (at least in your mind's eye) to be open-minded and open-hearted on the journey towards becoming a more competent and confident you?

   YES   NO   c. Are you willing to be more accountable in making and maintaining sustainable changes, even after you fall down?

   If you answered YES to any of these questions, then you are ready to go deeper in the questions you ask yourself to reach your goal.

2. Asking deeper questions requires you to look at places that cause you some discomfort. Although this may seem intimidating, being uncomfortable is the beginning of authentic learning. * However, years of disappointment in not breaking through the discomfort to find resolution can shut us down when we revisit these painful memories. To help gently nudge you forward, circle the commitment level you can realistically give at this time. As much as possible refrain from the temptation of self-judgment. See these questions as an attempt to raise your level of awareness. Circle a number representing your willingness to go deeper in fleshing out your authentic self, to "live your questions."

Note the three stages of increasing your awareness and commitment:

- Describing the facts but not the feelings ("I gained 50 pounds after I ended a relationship.")

- Clarifying gives feeling and facts but may veer towards rationalization ("I gained 50 pounds after I ended my last relationship. He was probably right when he said I think like an overweight person.")

- Being curious means looking at the situation nonjudgmentally ("I gained 50 pounds after I ended my last relationship. What's my real motivation to lose this weight now?")

DIRECTIONS: Circle the number (1 – 5, 5 high) that best represents your willingness to take a deeper look at yourself.

a. Do I self-sabotage after a disappointment (ex: weight loss, eating right, exercising, making more money, finding a right-fit job, finding a compatible partner, etc.)?

1 2 3 4 5

b. Does this situation mirror an unresolved aspect of myself?

1 2 3 4 5

c. Am I willing to look at how old mental messages or beliefs trip me up?

1 2 3 4 5

d. Am I willing to try new tools and strategies (empathy, grit, growth mindset) to help change unproductive behaviors and attitudes?

1 2 3 4 5

* Note: In cases of severe trauma, physically, psychologically, or psychically, these application activities are no substitute for the professional services of a licensed grief specialist or trauma counselor.

3. Conduct this thought exercise. Look at the horizontal line below. The right end of the line represents your fluid life, your abundant life, your life as you choose it in the

present moment from a "both/and" perspective. The left end of the line represents your fixed life with a focus on deficits and limitations, a life of indecision fixated on the past or future. These are symptoms of an "either/or" perspective. The solid line is what you already know; the dotted lines are what's unresolved, an unrealized memory from the past or expectation of the future.

— — — — ——————————————— — — — —

a. Place a fulcrum somewhere along the solid horizontal line as a representation of how you view your life unfolding. Be as honest and nonjudgmental as you can. If the fulcrum is not at the midpoint of the horizontal line— a rare event for most of us—ask yourself where you are committed to putting the fulcrum.

b. On which side of the fulcrum would you put the following questions:

- Am I giving a high priority to self-judgment?
- Can I be happy despite my perceived deficits?
- Can I quiet my mind when my "hot" button gets pushed?
- Do I display victim identity when something does not go my way?
- What opportunities lay hidden in the adversity surrounding me?

- Can I trust my instinct about my innate wisdom to pursue a healthy path?

- Can I show compassion to my emerging (and fragile) self when I make a mistake?

4. Are you willing to live the life you've imagined? If so, answer these questions that put you in the direction of your dreams:

   a. What happened today that made you keep going to satisfy unmet needs?

   b. What did you learn from that? What's your takeaway?

   c. What surprised you about how you responded to any mistakes you made?

   d. What strategy are you going to try to get back on track?

5. Now let's have another look at the questions you addressed in number 2. How might you answer these questions given an abundant perspective rather than a deficit perspective?

   a. What causes me to abandon my effort after a disappointment?

   b. How does this situation mirror an aspect of myself?

   c. What are my old (and new) mental messages or beliefs about this?

   d. What tools will help me with this situation?

6. Draw an image or make a collage of the new YOU reaching your goal. Select an image that is out of the ordinary. Make sure it is affirming your new sense of self. Make sure it is amazing!

Gratitude

This final section is about gratitude. Living a more vibrant life is about letting go of old and un-useful patterns and beliefs about yourself. Living a more vibrant life means finding the blessings despite the boulders on your path. Identifying your gratitude, often in the midst of discomfort, can open your eyes to see the unseen and rich blessings all around you. By acknowledging your empathy for yourself and others, you let go of any unproductive protections of your ego. You welcome moments of self-care that can open your heart to the fruits of compassion. By tapping into your grit, you let go of any hesitation or ambivalence and support perseverance and connection to your passion. By shifting from a fixed mindset to a growth mindset you let go of beliefs which no longer work for you as you move into new ways of thinking about yourself and your world. Don't be afraid to ask these important and hard questions. Face the fear. Feel the gratitude.

- At the surface layer: With every day I am thankful for _____

- Digging a little deeper: Even in my darkest hour I appreciate _____

- Now breaking through the hard rock protecting past hurts: When I don't edit or prejudge my motivations, I know my new way of life will be

  _____

Resources

GreatMasters

If you like the ideas in this book, please visit our website for program services and consultation options:
www.GreatMastersInc.com

Empathy

Baron-Cohen, Simon, *Zero Degrees of Empathy: The New Theory of Human Cruelty and Kindness*, Penguin, 2012

Brown, Brene, *Rising Strong: The Reckoning, The Rumble, The Revolution*, Penguin Random House, 2015

Brown, Brene, "The Power of Vulnerability," a TED talk, Jan 3, 2011, https://www.ted.com/talks/brene_brown_on_vulnerability#t-578185

McLaren, Karla, *The Art of Empathy: A Complete Guide to Life's Most Essential Skill*, Sounds True Audiotapes, 2013

Grit

Duckworth, Angela, *Grit: The Power of Passion and Perseverance*, Scribner, 2016

Hoerr, T., Fostering Grit: How Do I Prepare My Students for the Real World? ASCD Arias, 2013, p. 52.

Kaplan, Linda Kaplan and Koval, Robin, *Grit to Great: How Perseverance, Passion, and Pluck Take You from Ordinary to Extraordinary*, Thayer Crown Business; First Edition, 2015

Meadows, Martin, *Grit: How to Keep Going When You Want to Give Up*, CreateSpace Independent Publishing Platform, 2015

Sharrock, Daisy, *Down the Rabbit Hole: An Exploration of Student Grit*, CreateSpace Independent Publishing Platform, 2013

Tough, Paul, *How Children Succeed: Grit, Curiosity, and the Hidden Power of Character*, Houghton Mifflin Harcourt, 2012

Mindset:

Dweck, Carol, *Mindset: The New Psychology of Success*, Random House, 2006

FourWaystoDevelopGrowthMindset,http://growingleaders.com/blog/four-ways-to-develop-a-growth-mindset/

Hogan, Milana L., *The Power of Grit and Growth*, Chief Learning Officer, August 1, 2014

Hughson, Barbara, *Grit, and the Growth Mindset in Family Law Meditation: A Qualitative Inquiry*, ERIC, 2014

Motivate Students to Grow Their Mindset, http://www.mindsetworks.com/

Study Smarter ebook, http://inkwellscholars.org/study-smarter/

Questions, Consciousness and Calling

Bayda, Ezra, *The Authentic Life: Zen Wisdom for Living Free from Complacency and Fear*, Shambhala, 2014

Griscom, Chris, *The Ageless Body*, The Light Institute Press, 1992

Heward, Lyn and Bacon, John U., *Cirque du Soleil: The Spark: Igniting the Creativity Fire that Lives Within Us All*, Currency Doubleday, 2006

Levoy, Gregg, *Callings: Finding and Following an Authentic Life*, Three Rivers Press, 1997

McDonnell, Karl, *It's All in Your Mind*, Chief Learning Officer, August 20, 2014

Richards, M. C., *Centering: In Pottery, Poetry, and the Person*, University Press of New England, 1989

Tolle, Eckhart, *Stillness Speaks*, New World Library, 2003

Acknowledgements

This is a book about staying awake despite the temptations all around me to be lulled back to sleep, to revert to automatic pilot. My deepest thanks go to my students, past and present. They are my true mentors and have kept me on my toes, creating so many opportunities for teachable and learnable moments. This book is also about showing up, every day, with the freshest version of myself. That can be scary, to trust the shadowy images of my emerging self. So, my numero uno gratitude, for recognizing the gem amidst the pebbles, I give my bottomless thanks to Sue who believed in me and gently reoriented me when I enthusiastically embraced half-baked ideas.

Dr. Wayne Benenson

When I began my dissertation journey many years ago, I had no clue that the ideas I'd researched would turn into this book. Again, and I again, I learned the lesson of following my instincts and not letting feelings of insecurity hold me back. Thank you, thank you to my family and friends who supported me through the challenges and joys of my doctoral journey. Special thanks go to the members of my dissertation committee who believed in me even when I didn't. They modeled greatness for me!

Dr. Barb Hughson

Authors' Biographies

Wayne Benenson, Ph.D., has been a teacher in variety of classrooms for 50 years, as an early childhood and an elementary school teacher, as a trainer in school-based peer mediation and Social Emotional Learning strategies, and as a college professor (undergraduate and graduate levels) in Education. Currently, he teaches mindfulness classes online to help students and adults cope with isolation, calm emotional dysregulation and manage distractions. He lives in Phoenix, Arizona and never tires of Sonoran Desert sunsets.

Barb Hughson, Ed.D., is a leadership coach, consultant, and trainer. She has used her degrees, a MA, and a MS. Ed. in Dance and Counseling and Education, and an Ed.D. in Organizational Leadership, to further her passions as a family mediator and therapist for children and adolescents. For over 20 years she has been an online instructor at various colleges and universities across the country teaching psychology, sociology, and business/leadership courses to both undergraduate and graduate students. She loves working with leaders to guide them to a better version of themselves.